How We Write Now

BLACK FEMINISM ON THE EDGE

Jennifer C. Nash

HOW WE WRITE NOW

Living with Black Feminist Theory

DUKE UNIVERSITY PRESS
Durham and London
2024

Project Editor: Bird Williams
Designed by A. Mattson Gallagher
Typeset in Garamond Premier Pro by Westchester Publishing
Services

Library of Congress Cataloging-in-Publication Data
Names: Nash, Jennifer C., [date] author.
Title: How we write now : living with Black feminist theory /
Jennifer C. Nash.
Other titles: Black feminism on the edge.
Description: Durham : Duke University Press, 2024. | Series: Black
feminism on the edge series | Includes bibliographical references
and index.
Identifiers: LCCN 2023040663 (print)
LCCN 2023040664 (ebook)
ISBN 9781478030461 (paperback)
ISBN 9781478026235 (hardcover)
ISBN 9781478059509 (ebook)
Subjects: LCSH: Nash, Jennifer C., 1980—Family. | African
American feminists. | African American women authors. | African
American authors. | African American mothers in literature. |
Feminist literature—United States. | Feminist literary criticism—
United States. | Feminist theory—United States. | BISAC: SOCIAL
SCIENCE / Ethnic Studies / American / African American & Black
Studies | LITERARY CRITICISM / Semiotics & Theory
Classification: LCC HQ1197 . N38 2024 (print)
LCC HQ11977 (ebook)
DDC 305.42089/96—dc23/eng/20240124
LC record available at https://lccn.loc.gov/2023040663
LC ebook record available at https://lccn.loc.gov/2023040664

Cover art: Laura James, *Upstairs*, 2005. Acrylic on canvas,
81.3 × 58.4 cm. © Laura James. All Rights Reserved 2024/
Bridgeman Images.

My loss was a tender second skin.

JESMYN WARD

*

I pray my mama don't forget about me.

NONAME

CONTENTS

ix   Preface: Beauty, or All about My Mother

xiii   Acknowledgments

1
1   Beauty, or All about
Black Feminist Theory's Mothers

2
25   Staying at the Bone

3
48   An Invitation to Listen

4
69   Picturing Loss

91   Conclusion: New Furniture, or
All about Black Feminist Theory's Fathers

99   Notes

117   Bibliography

127   Index

In the time it takes me to write this book, my mother may lose her capacity to read this sentence. Every morning when I meet this work, I write against the cruel force of that realization.

This book's opening sentence contains the conditional: this *may* happen. Everything that conventional medicine has to tell us about Alzheimer's—which is surprisingly little—and how it manifests in those who are diagnosed before their sixty-fifth birthday suggests that my mother's near future holds steady cognitive deterioration. Our world comes to be shaped by statistics and risk assessments; we try to predict something about which predictions are likely to be faulty. We wait. We hope. We monitor. And in the midst of this, we live.

Through a combination of something I can only call luck and the immense generosity of a cadre of colleagues, in the third year of my mother's living-with Alzheimer's, I find myself working at an institution that is twenty minutes from my parents.[1] For the first time in my adult life, I live in the same city as them. I have grown tired of the "frenzied rituals of academic legitimation," rituals that have, at times, led me to places where I have not wanted to live—or to places I *thought* I wanted to live, only to discover I didn't.[2] The endless choreography of packing and moving, settling and orienting, has been in the service of credentialization. I have also told myself it has been in the name of a certain kind of freedom, inching toward more time and space for the things that I hold dearest, namely, writing every day. But there is a kind of fatigue that academics spend too little time describing, one perhaps more profound for faculty of color, who—in a moment that continues to be marked by anti-Blackness and our peculiar fetishization and valuation in a marketplace structured by diversity's relentless logics—are moved, traded, shuffled, in an endless game of musical chairs whose results are announced each year on Twitter and Instagram. The previous sentence is not entirely true. We move ourselves. We shuffle ourselves. But we are also moved and shuffled by institutions who promise us *more*: freedom, time, money, autonomy. This all hides something that I think too often goes unnamed in academia: loneliness. *Gratitude* is too small a word to describe what I feel when I find myself simply watching the annual academic musical chairs, the elaborate dance of moving institutions, packing offices, and announcing new titles. I sit this one out, not out of resignation or disappointment, but out of something that academia has not taught me to recognize: contentment.

My parents have a key to our house, and at least three times a week, they stop by. We eat dinner together. We go for walks. We buy each other toilet paper from Target. We change each other's light bulbs, pick up each other's dry cleaning, ferry small boxes of food to each other's houses. This, to me, epitomizes what Christina Sharpe calls "sounding an ordinary note of care."[3] We don't sound it, though. We simply do it. And we do it again and again. In doing it, in repeating it, we make it.

But my mother's diagnosis and the slow pace at which these words are written means that this book might not reach her, or it won't reach her the way I want it to. I use the word *might* because I do not yet know if this project is an attempt to catch her—preserve her—in a moment when there are parts of her that are still recognizable to me, or if this is an effort to mourn her even as this loss is still unfolding. Perhaps, I admit to myself, there is some relief in the fact that this project will not make it to her. My mother would not like the fact of this book. She would not want to find herself the subject of my inquiry, and she certainly would feel some shame at the condition of her memory described in an academic text. I have struggled with what disclosure means for her as we navigate social spaces together—my father and I endlessly assess who needs to know about her diagnosis, until we reach a point when we realize that even if we do not disclose her diagnosis, it is already obvious—and as I navigate my own intellectual interests, which have always been shaped by the conditions of my ordinary life. Sharpe tells us that "there are other stories to tell here, but they're not mine to tell."[4] It is hard for me to ascertain which stories belong to me and what ownership means when we talk about the complicated entanglements of family history. I can't discern the difference between her story and mine, the boundary between where her life ends and mine begins.

Now there is simply the magnitude of loss, and its long duration. I live my life imagining what it will be to lose her, and with that loss slowly unfolding. I watch her face, carefully record her answers to questions, always, I realize, wondering one thing: What will happen if—when—she forgets me?[5] This is what you should know about me: I bring to this project a dense set of desires for my mother to live on in a form that is familiar to me.[6] I know those desires will not be met. This is the critical and affective energy that animates this book.

I often sit in the uncomfortable space between the theoretical work I teach and my embodied experience. Perhaps many of us do, measuring the complexity of existence by the distance between the text and the body, between the word and the lived. I try to name this space for my students, but I find I often fail to do justice to it with words. I can explain it here like this: I spend this past semester reading feminist texts with graduate students. We circle again and again around the limits of generational logic for feminist inquiry and imagine the possibilities of anti-generational feminist thinking. We talk about the "stories" feminists have told and about feminists' enduring preoccupation with telling time in ways that uphold normative logics of kinship.[7]

I hold secret that I am still seduced by this logic, that the idea of generationality structures my thinking and living in profound ways. I come to write about my mother only after I have a daughter. I feel an invisible thread woven around the three of us, and I feel it tighten as the years pass. We are three generations of only children. We are three generations of only girls. If I let that thread weave one generation back, I see my mother's mother, my grandmother, also an only child. I barely knew her. By the time I was old enough to be curious about her existence, she had already been diagnosed with Alzheimer's, and she managed it by retreating from anything that we might call social life. I remember a conversation I overheard where she confessed to my mother—her daughter—that she thought I feared her, that I was uncomfortable around the lapses in her memory, the questions she repeated, the long stares she would cast in my direction as if trying to memorize my face. I was ashamed, and I tried to channel that shame into a kind of contrived generosity. I sat with her. I held her hand. I tried desperately to find a way to comfort her. But I was too young to understand the sheer pain of a grandmother who felt that the granddaughter right in front of her could not see her. She felt herself disappearing. Or, perhaps worse, that I was disappearing her. Now, nearly thirty years later, as I "gather my ghosts," I realize that I have to contend with this history as part of what binds our four generations.[8] These women are in the room with me as I write, as is my daughter, sitting across the table from me, staring at me with dark eyes that are a mirror image of my own.

ACKNOWLEDGMENTS

This book has been made possible by the kindness of the people I hold dearest.

I owe more than I can say to Samantha Pinto, my ride or die and my treasured writing and thinking companion. I thank her for all the times she read this and helped me find a way forward. I am also grateful for our ongoing conversation, for a year of walks around the mid-major, and for the many collaborations that remind me why I do this thing.

Thanks to Emily Owens, my beloved sister, forever homegirl, and deeply generous reader. We started a conversation in the Gato Rojo two decades ago, and we've been talking ever since: celebrating books and babies, exchanging ideas and pages, supporting each other through all of life's challenges and complexities, and chatting about the wondrous stuff of the everyday.

Robyn Wiegman, my dear friend and trusted mentor, read many drafts of these chapters and met their incompletion with her incomparable brilliance, rigor, and willingness to believe in the possible. I am especially grateful for everything she has taught me about feminist institution building, for the way she has made Duke an intellectual home for me, and for the doors she has generously opened at every step of my professional life.

I owe so much to Mishana Garschi, editorial GOAT, queen of all details, and George to my Jerry. I am thankful for her smart feedback, her brilliant editing and copious indexing, and a treasured friendship cemented over cookies, escapes from Evanston, veggie samplers, and *Seinfeld* references.

When I walked into my first day of a new job in 2010, I had the tremendously good fortune of meeting Katie Rademacher Kein. We spent the first six years of our friendship as two kids navigating American studies. We have spent the last eight years as two kids navigating feminist pedagogy, parenting, and our ongoing attempts to predict who will win March Madness. I am grateful for the many years of daily texts and for her wise and generous feedback on this manuscript.

Thanks to my colleagues in Gender, Sexuality, and Feminist studies and friends at Duke University. I owe special thanks to Jolie Olcott—my extraordinarily supportive department chair during my first years at Duke—for friendship and walks, and for Making Things Happen.

Thanks to Durham friends: Chaunesti Webb, Lisa Levenstein, Lauren Henschel, Suzanne Katzenstein, Paniz Musawi Natanzi, Julien Fischer (Duo family), Pete Sigal, Emily Wang, and Sarah Jane Cervenak. Thanks to Anna Storti, Emily Wang, and Pete Sigal for reading an earlier version of this work and offering helpful feedback.

Thanks to friends from the many places that have been home: Durba Mitra, Justin Mann, Jonathan Evans, Amy Siniscalchi, Peter Geller, Amber Musser, Ramzi Fawaz, Meghan Morris and Nate Ela (Chicago family), Attiya Ahmad, Marquis Bey, Emily Hirsch, Tom Guglielmo, and my beloved *co-madre* Maria Duran Pino.

Thank you to my students for asking questions that keep me thinking. And many thanks to the generous participants in the Black Feminist Theory Summer Institute at Duke University in 2022 and 2023 for collectively forging a generative space. I learned so much from moving exchanges with Kevin Quashie, Samantha Pinto, Emily Owens, La Marr Jurelle Bruce, Justin Mann, LaMonda Horton-Stallings, Sharon Holland, Sarah Jane Cervenak, Erica Edwards, Jovonna Jones, Tiffany Lethabo King, Sherie Randolph, Mercy Romero, Bianca Williams, Marquis Bey, Antonia Randolph, and Danielle Purifoy, and from engagement with two cohorts of incredibly brilliant graduate students. Thank you is too small for what I owe Kevin Quashie, not just for the gift of his beautiful scholarship, but also for his generous engagement with my work at the Summer Institute and beyond.

Duke University Press has been a central part of my intellectual life, and I am grateful for the labor and intellectual commitments of everyone there. Thank you to the anonymous readers who offered their smart feedback on earlier versions of this work. And many thanks to Elizabeth Ault for generous intellectual conversations and lunches from Toast.

Many thanks to my teachers: Liz Roncka for much-needed doses of pandemic Pilates sanity, and Adeline Sussman for many hours spent in the studio working steadily on the practice and helping me keep my mind and body strong.

Thank you to *Signs* for publishing an earlier version of this work, to *Lit Hub* for an opportunity to write personally about loss and family history, and to *Boston Review* (especially Adam McGee) for space to try out ideas that are developed here.

Thanks to my family:

Thanks to the ones who came before me whom I carry in my heart. I keep telling stories about them so that they can live on in my daughter's heart.

My father, Douglas Nash, has traveled with me to this terrain we didn't expect to inhabit, with grace and patience, with good humor and an unyielding commitment to his family. More than that, he has supported me in every way imaginable and taught me so much about the small acts of daily care that underpin love.

This book was motivated—from beginning to end—by a desire to hold my mother, Carolyn Nash, close. I carried her in my mind and heart each morning when I met this work. I am grateful for her affection and her beautiful spirit.

Mom and Dad, thank you is far too small to express my gratitude for your loving presence in every single day of my life. All I can say is come over on Sunday and I'll make you some salmon.

Thanks to Amar (BBD) Ahmad for knowing when to get deep and when to keep it light, for delightfully quirky animations, and for our precious friendship.

Thanks to Naima Ahmad Nash for modeling what it means to be brave, bold, and deeply open to the world. She has opened my heart wider than I ever imagined, taught me that growth and change are possible, and reminded me that kitchen dance parties and macaron afternoons are the stuff of everyday magic. Because she asked for it: "Naima, I love you, more every time."

This book was made possible by Amin Ahmad's steady love. I thank him for getting me, for always knowing how to make me laugh, for sanity walks and cuddles, and for the millions of small gestures that show his affection. More than anything, I thank him for the gift of his companionship and the pleasure of spending every day talking to each other. The years pass, the memories multiply, the roots deepen, the adventures continue, the love grows, and we hold on to one simple philosophy: *twenty years, one mic.*

1

Beauty, or All about
Black Feminist Theory's Mothers

This book begins with my mother's story. But if I am honest, the book is entirely about her, and the experience of losing her in slow motion. It is certainly about what it has meant for me to mother my own daughter while I watch my mother begin to forget herself, and maybe, one day, me.[1]

This book is also about a Black feminist frame of Black loss, and the voice through which that frame has been developed, circulated, and honed with a particular intensity in the period of Black Lives Matter. This frame has allowed a broad public to understand Black loss and Black survival as tethered to Black mothers and their "wake work."[2] This archive includes Claudia Rankine's "'The Condition of Black Life Is One of Mourning,'" published in the *New York Times Magazine* in 2015, where Rankine diagnoses the regularity—the ordinariness—of Black loss by describing how expected loss constitutes Black maternal life. She writes, "A friend recently told me that when she gave birth to her son, before naming him, before even nursing him, her first thought was, I have to get him out of this country."[3] She then describes another conversation with a friend about "what it's like being the mother of a black son. 'The condition of black life is one of mourning,' she said bluntly. For her, mourning lived in real time inside her and her son's reality: At any moment she might lose her reason for living." For Rankine, bereaved Black mothers are icons of Black loss, symbols of anticipation, always, as Elizabeth Alexander describes, "sleep[ing] with one eye open."[4] This profound sense of burden has rendered Black mothers, following Brenda Tindal's insights, the "movement widows" of this era who "enter the national imagination . . . through the mortality and martyrdom of black boys and men."[5] And so there is a particular form of loss—the expected, sudden, and spectacular murder of Black boys and men at the hands of the state—that has come to be understood, thanks to the tremendously important intellectual and political labor of Black feminists, as the paradigmatic form of Black loss.[6]

But this framework has made a host of other ordinary forms of Black loss invisible, or at least illegible as *Black*. Those are the losses this book is interested in. Let me be more specific: I remember an early visit to the neurologist when my mother's doctor asked us how my mother manages her symptoms. We described the millions of small strategies she has developed to continue to participate in social life. She can nod empathically during a conversation to give the appearance of following along; she can turn her lips downward at what she imagines to be a tragic turn in a speaker's story. She is a skilled reader of social cues, and the doctor celebrates this as a sign of her cognitive health. The doctor called this behavior *masking* and reminded us that when my mother has grown unable or unwilling to hide the gaps in her memory, we will know that her Alzheimer's is truly advancing.

My mother is a child of the Black middle class. Her father taught English at Brooklyn College, and her mother was a high school math teacher. Her parents valued books, discipline, and rigor (perhaps more than affection—though as their only grandchild and, as the family narrative went, the inheritor of my grandfather's penchant for academic pursuits, I only ever saw their tenderness). As a child, I would watch my mother construct her flawless face every morning before she would head to work.[7] She would curl her hair and paint her lips a deep burgundy. I was aware, even as a child, that she was shielding everything I knew—and could never fully know—about who she was from the world that she navigated. I am aware now, as an adult, that she was also always bracing herself for impact; she was anticipating the forms of everyday racial and gendered conflict that marked her life as a Black woman moving through the space of the hospital, the place where she worked for over two decades. Her professional mask aspired to shield what Kevin Quashie describes as "the full range of [her] inner life—one's desires, ambitions, hunger, vulnerabilities, fears"—from the regularity and ordinariness of violence that marked her workplace.[8] Perhaps this is why her brain has fiercely clung to masking. I am not sure what it might mean for her to lose this "skill," but I know that I can only think of this future and seemingly inevitable loss as a Black one even as it falls outside of the frame of Black loss that Black feminists have developed—one that centers predictable forms of anti-Black state violence. This book insists that the framework of Black loss that Black feminists advance abandons an account of the Black ordinary, and the forms of loss that are embedded there.[9]

In this book I use the term *loss* to capture Black feminists' theorization of a meta-temporality that includes multiple and overlapping forms of affect and time—waiting, anticipation, the chronic, the durational—all of which decenter the primacy of the event and instead focus on the quotidian, the experiences of sitting with and living in loss. And I describe various, and intersecting, forms of loss that unfold on numerous scales. At times, loss registers as grief, transition, change, trauma, newness, unfamiliarity. Loss can be of people, of love, of objects, of stability, of familiarity, of places, of history. Loss can be intimate, political, social, and it is often lived and felt at the places where these scales intersect. Loss can be welcome, it can be unbearable, and it can trigger mixed feelings and ambivalence. And loss can be anticipated—something that structures present time by its imagined (or real) certainty—or it can be disarming in its sudden appearance. If I inflect loss so broadly, what coheres the various experiences I write about here is a relationship to time that upends the "chrononormative," that can make time collapse, expand, or turn on itself.[10]

In flagging loss—and thus the endured—as a significant part of how Black feminist theorists have imagined and represented Black female subjectivities, I am not upholding still-prevalent "controlling images" of Black female strength—what Joan Morgan famously called the image of the "strongblackwoman"—that treat Black women as impervious to pain.[11] Nor am I offering a conception of Black women as long-suffering, or as always already grieving. Instead, I contend that contemporary Black feminist theory disrupts prevailing conceptions of loss that, as David Eng and David Kazanjian advance, treat the question of loss as animated by another question: "What remains?"[12] This suggests that there is loss and its afterlife, that loss is an event that splits temporality into a before and after.[13] This conception of loss presumes that what was lost was once possessed, that its absence is evidence of non-ownership or even of theft. Black feminist writing on loss reveals that there is no difference between the remains and the lost; life is lived in and through loss. And it also shows that ownership and possession are complex fictions for Black people generally, and Black women specifically. This book asks: What does it mean to lose something that was only ever partially yours? I pose this question in the context of the place I write from. I know that I come to this project with a desire to fix my mother in a moment when her very self seems to be changing in front of my eyes, when she is becoming unfamiliar to me. I have had to come to terms with all I never asked her, and all I will never get a chance to ask her. I have spent far too many hours seeking to master her story and thus to feel I have some mastery over my own, only to realize that a life story—or stories—cannot be pinned down. I know now that honoring parts of my mother's life that are opaque might be to grant her what I hope my daughter will one day grant me—privacy.[14]

How We Write Now maintains that the paradigmatic form of Black loss that Black feminists have made visible is articulated through a singular kind of voice. Indeed, contemporary Black feminist theory insists that theory has a voice—or *should* have a voice. It is an affectively saturated voice, a deliberately revelatory voice, a voice that discloses, truth-tells, and stays close to the bone. It is a voice that is deployed to make visible what Black loss *feels* like, how it moves under the skin, how it shapes Black inner lives, how it organizes Black sociality *and* interiority.[15] This voice speaks in an intimate register; it grapples with the ethics of disclosure, the risk of saying too much or too little. This is writing that willingly bears the chance of meeting a reader who exclaims: "All this emotional stuff just leaves me cold," and does nothing to mitigate that risk.[16] This voice intentionally speaks intimately to its reader—we might even think of it as whispering to its reader—with an attention to language that is poetic, with an investment in how words sound when they are read or heard, and with a commitment to the fact that words are always more than words, that books are more than books, that Black feminist theory can, *does*, "save our lives."[17] Contemporary Black feminist texts insist that the act of writing and reading Black feminist theory can be—or, perhaps, *should* be—an act of care, "wake work," "defending the dead," "gathering the ghosts," and "taking our dead with us to the various battles we must wage in their names—and in our own names."[18] This body of writing carries with it a sense of the profundity and magnitude of what Black women have lost, not in the hopes of reparation or recuperation, but in the service of naming the always-already-thereness of loss at various scales as constitutive of Black women's lives. It is a voice that is not just documentary in its capacity to record the felt life of grief but also pedagogical in its capacity to offer tools for living with and living on.

Beautiful. That is the term I have landed on to name the singular Black feminist voice that I describe—and at times deploy—here.

I use the amorphous and slippery term *beautiful* to characterize certain writing practices, though I do not mean beautiful as a form of valuation. Instead, I use it to describe the aesthetic properties of contemporary Black feminist theoretical work and to capture its ethical commitments, particularly its aspiration to move the reader, even as it might move the reader in a variety of ways or may not move the reader at all. This writing also provokes unmoved readers to perform the work of asking why they remain unmoved, to probe what might make them feel for—and with—the authors that perform this kind of writing.[19] I use the term *beautiful* to capture repetition, including the now ubiquity of certain forms (the letter) and representations (the photograph) in Black feminist theoretical writing that allow their authors to whisper in their readers' ears. These repeated forms and commitments to disclosure reveal that Black feminist theorists are invested in modes of writing that are, as Patricia J. Williams notes, "an act of sacrifice, not denial. . . . What is 'impersonal' writing but denial of self?"[20] Black feminist theorists mobilize their prose to ask readers to feel, to make us feel otherwise, to undo us, and, sometimes, to reassemble us. I suggest that *how Black feminists write now* is in a beautiful voice, one that we find essential to staying close to what has become our central preoccupation: loss. In making the claim that beautiful writing is central to contemporary Black feminist theory's investment in loss, I am also insisting that Black feminist theorists treat loss as, in part, an aesthetic question. Black feminist theorists show that an intimacy with loss recalibrates our understanding of the regularity and massiveness of loss, and its quiet, ordinary iterations and reverberations.

This beautiful voice is one that I take on in this book even as this very voice is the book's object of study. I confess: I am seduced by this voice and its commitment to a proximity between its authors and their objects, between its authors and readers, even as I am deeply interested in how and why seduction has become important to contemporary Black feminist writing. I use the term *seduction* differently than other Black feminist writers, as when Saidiya Hartman describes it as the "violence obscured by the veil."[21] When I say I am seduced by beautiful writing, I track how this writing works on me both as a reader and as a writer. As a reader, I imagine that this form of writing brings me closer to the truth of something, that its refusal of distance transports me to the messy complexity of loss and its endless reverberations. As a writer, I think about how this form of writing gets under a reader's skin.

Since loss often eludes its own telling, I am curious about the promise that beautiful writing contains—that it can bring us closer to a truth of loss. I treat this assurance—alongside the fact that proximity often yields more mystery—as the seductive work of beautiful writing. Even as the voice that Black feminist theory has honed promises to take us to the scene of loss and to keep us there, to get us as close to loss as possible, loss remains a slippery object that troubles memory and evades capture.

You will see throughout this book my own explorations with contemporary Black feminist theory's dominant voice: I write about my mother. I write about my daughter. And I write in a voice that—for me—feels different from the one that appears in my earlier work. I suppose I have surrendered something in writing this book: perhaps it is the armor of critical distance, and the privacy that assembling evidence and argumentation has always afforded me. But I felt I couldn't write this book without this voice, even as I am hungry to explore both its propulsive power and its shortcomings. What this book does, then, is to offer a conceptual framework for thinking about contemporary Black feminist writing's commitment to sitting with and at the scene of loss through beautiful writing.

How

Christina Sharpe's account of beauty begins with her mother.

She tells her readers, "I learned to see in my mother's house. I learned how not to see in my mother's house. How to limit my sight to the things that could be controlled. I learned to see in discrete angles, planes, plots. If the ceiling was falling down and you couldn't do anything about it, what you could do was grow and arrange peonies and tulips and zinnias; cut forsythia and mock orange to bring inside."[22] Like Alice Walker, one of the preeminent Black feminist theorists of the garden, Sharpe reminds us that the tulips and the zinnias, the peonies and the forsythia, are a manifestation of a Black maternal commitment to beauty-making, to what Hartman describes as "creating possibility in the space of enclosure."[23]

For Sharpe, beauty enables imagining escape *and* staying put. Beauty engenders forms of movement, transporting her from "the windowsill to the world."[24] As she narrates, "My mother gave me space to dream. For whole days at a time, she left me with and to words, curled up in a living-room windowsill, uninterrupted in my reading and imagining other worlds."[25] But beauty also makes possible Sharpe's closeness to the room, to the specific "angles, planes, [and] plots" that her mother taught her both to see and unsee. Beauty is a method of seeing our "mothers' gardens"—whether in a plot of earth or on a windowsill—as providing a blueprint for living.

Elizabeth Alexander's account of beauty begins with a Black maternal gaze.

Alexander's sustained meditation on the "Trayvon Generation"—a term she introduced in a *New Yorker* article in 2020 when the US was marked by the urgency and strange slowness of pandemic temporality and by a new racial "reckoning" engendered by George Floyd's murder—describes her sons, her students, and the young people who have come of age with stories of Black death "instruct[ing them] . . . about their embodiment and their vulnerability. The stories were primers in fear and futility."[26] She portrays the depression, the anxious anticipation, and the ordinariness of grief that have come to mark this cohort. Her essay—her diagnosis—is written from her position as a mother, as a Black mother, who has a single wish: "I want my children—all of them—to thrive, to be fully alive. How do we measure what that means? What does it mean for our young people to be 'black alive and looking back at you . . . ?'"[27]

But her essay ends not with an(other) image of Black suffering but instead with an image of Black beauty: dance.[28] Or, more precisely, it ends with her watching her sons dance together. She writes:

> I measure my success as a mother of black boys in part by the fact that I have sons who love to dance, who dance in community, who dance till their powerful bodies sweat, who dance and laugh, who dance and shout. Who are able—in the midst of their studying and organizing, their fear, their rage, their protesting, their vulnerability, their missteps and triumphs, their knowledge that they must fight the hydra-headed monster of racism and racial violence that we were not able to cauterize—to find the joy and the power of communal self-expression . . . People dance to say, *I am alive and in my body. I am black alive and looking back at you.*[29]

Even as she insists that "this essay is not a celebration, nor is it an elegy" that dance itself will not free us," Alexander leaves her readers with movement as a symbol of Black personhood, vitality, and living.[30] And while Alexander's conception of children and parents, Black sons and Black mothers, exceeds the logics of biological reproduction, she also insists that beauty is about an anticipatory Black maternal gaze that might be briefly calmed by seeing Black boys dancing.

For me, an account of beauty begins with my mother folding laundry.

My mother is now most herself—or so it seems to me—when she gleefully empties a hamper of clean clothes onto the bed. She shakes each garment until it lets out a crackle. She presses the fabric with the palms of her hands, working out each wrinkle with her fingers. She reshapes crumpled, tired cotton into crisp squares and triangles. I sense that she feels an ease in not having to talk, a comforting simplicity in the repetition of shaking, smoothing, bending, creasing. In a moment when she is becoming unfamiliar to me—and perhaps I am becoming unfamiliar to her—I see her insistence on loving me through these small acts of organizing and arranging. I see in the banality of this act something I can only think of as maternal tenderness.

If this book makes the claim that beautiful Black feminist writing is a voice developed and honed to allow Black feminists to stay close to loss, I insist that much of the work of staying close to loss has required staying close to mothers. Black feminists often narrate loss through the figure of Black mothers: lost Black mothers, grieving Black mothers, lost Black motherlands, the losses that Black mothers attempt to mitigate through ordinary practices of tenderness and care, and the losses that attend to—and are imagined to attend to—Black maternal life, particularly, as I argue in my earlier book, in a moment where Black mother and grief have become synonymous.[31] Saidiya Hartman's *Lose Your Mother*, Hortense Spillers's "Mama's Baby, Papa's Maybe," Christina Sharpe's *Ordinary Notes*, Alice Walker's *In Search of Our Mothers' Gardens*, Alexis Pauline Gumbs's *Revolutionary Mothering*, and Patricia J. Williams's "search" for her great-great-grandmother's history that inaugurates *The Alchemy of Race and Rights*, are all part of a larger Black feminist archive that centers theorizing mothers, mothering, maternal labor, and the political life of Black motherhood as central to what Williams terms "self-possession . . . the companion to self-knowledge."[32] For Williams—and for a host of other Black feminist scholars—the labor of self-knowledge is the project of "searching for our mothers' gardens."[33] Four decades after Walker penned her canonical essay, Marquis Bey insists that "we are still searching for our mothers' gardens."[34] In making the claim that mothers are central to contemporary Black feminist theory's commitments, I find myself traveling alongside Walker's insistence that "so many of the stories that I write, that we all write, are my mother's stories. Only recently did I fully realize this: that through years of listening to my mother's stories of her life, I have absorbed not only the stories themselves, but something of the manner in which she spoke, something of the urgency that involves the knowledge that her stories—like her life—must be recorded."[35] What might it mean, this project asks, to think about how many of Black feminism's "stories"—particularly about loss—are about mothers and mothering, about maternal labor and maternal grief?

Even in a moment where to speak of mothers is to run the risk of being cast as pathologically passé and dangerously biologist, Black feminist theory has never surrendered its mothers and has become even more invested in mothers, as is evidenced by Sharpe's most recent *Ordinary Notes*, which Sharpe describes as a "love letter" to her mother, a love letter that also insists, "I wanted to write about *silences* and *terror* and acts that hover over generations, over centuries. I began by writing about my mother and grandmother."[36] The *now* that is in the title of this book—a now that I talk about in more detail later in this introduction—is marked by a proliferation of work that speaks in a deeply intimate voice about Black mothers and Black children, and about how a grammar of loss binds them to each other, and about how loss constitutes Black maternal subjectivity. To write Black loss, contemporary Black feminist theory tells us, is to write about the intimate lifeworlds of the Black maternal, which are imagined as constituted by proximity to grief that is always about to come, even as the temporality of loss gets mapped differently across this work, from the sudden anticipated grief of Black mothers to the grief that I want to map, slowly unfolding and of an unknown duration.

I began this section with Sharpe's celebration of her mother's investment in beauty, her commitment to "mak[ing] a small path through the wake."[37] Sharpe's essay is a tribute to attention, to noticing a mother's attempts at cross-stitch, appliqué, homemade Christmas ornaments, and a "perfect arrangement of pins."[38] But what if we sit not just with the *what* of Sharpe's enumeration of beauty as Black maternal method but the *how*: how she carefully attends to ordinary detail, how she slows down to notice a "neat paper log" rolled to keep a family warm or the roundness of her mother's cursive.[39] For Sharpe, beauty is:

> reading in the windowsill
> running after the police
> a list on a slip of paper in a book
> the arrangement of pins in cloth
> the ability to make firewood out of newspaper[40]

Beauty is a poem. It is a form of writing sensitive and sensitized to ordinary practices of tenderness, daily acts of living, breathing, and life-making that move Black people "from the windowsill to the world." It is a kind of writing that bridges genres to offer a loving and literary attention to the Black ordinary. It is also a manifesto that speaks to beauty as a mode of Black feminist writing and not merely a mode of Black feminist living.

Beauty emerges in contemporary Black feminist theory in multiple ways: at times, a way of describing language and its luxuriousness, its poiesis, its delightful excesses, its sensuality. This is a form of beauty where Black feminist theorists sit with—delight in sitting with—their objects, lingering with them, taking the time not merely to describe but to patiently attend to them. There is a temporality to this work: it is slow. But beauty does other work as well—at times, it refers to an arrangement, as when Sharpe notes, "What is beauty made of? Attentiveness whenever possible to a kind of aesthetic that escaped violence whenever possible—even if it is only the perfect arrangement of pins."[41] And at times, the insistence on Black beauty is an insistence on the beautifulness of Blackness.

Rather than treating the *effects* of this writing as beauty—though there is that too—I study beauty as a Black feminist method and, more particularly, an ethical method of Black feminist writing. When I describe it as an ethical method of writing, I mean that it takes emotional risks in the service of bringing its reader and writer closer to something: the scene of loss. In making the claim that beautiful writing aspires for proximity and intimacy, I am well aware of the illusory nature of both of these things—in seeking to get us closer to the truth of something, beautiful writing can fail or falter. It can misremember, it can romanticize, it can aspire to get at the heart of something only to find that "memory's false as anything."[42] But what I describe here as an ethics of writing centers contemporary Black feminist theory's will to *move* its reader, and contemporary Black feminist theorists' insistent push to get under their readers' skin. I see this as an ethical impulse because it insists that being moved—as in affected, and as in transported *by words* to the scene of loss—is a form of doing justice to loss. Of course, authors can never be certain of how their writing will move—or will not move—readers. As Ruth Behar writes in her engagement with vulnerable ethnographies, "Writing vulnerably takes as much skill, nuance, and willingness to follow through on all the ramifications of a complicated idea as does writing invulnerably and distantly. I would say it takes yet greater skill. The worst that can happen in an invulnerable text is that it will be boring. But when an author has made herself or himself vulnerable, the stakes are higher: a boring self-revelation, one that fails to move the reader, is more than embarrassing; it is humiliating."[43] This uncertainty might be one of the risks at the heart of beautiful writing, and it is this willingness to risk vulnerability, disclosure, and revelation in the service of potentially transforming its reader that may well be what makes this writing politically and ethically useful.

I am not alone in my attention to the relationship between Black feminist writing and beauty. Hartman's celebrated *Wayward Lives, Beautiful Experiments*—which I study at length in the pages that follow—treats beauty as a central analytic. The book is also written beautifully, through an unprecedented commitment to poetic language as crucial to honoring Black women's freedom dreams and practices of living.[44] Hartman merges critical fabulation and poetry, producing a series of scenes and "characters" whose lives she describes with an attention to the splendor of the ordinary. Hartman also emphasizes beauty as a practice of Black women's living, a strategy for securing some modicum of freedom. Her book celebrates young Black women who, at the turn of the twentieth century, "struggled to create autonomous and beautiful lives, to escape the new forms of servitude awaiting them, and to live as if they were free."[45] Hartman's investment in Black women's practices of living as "beautiful experiments to make living an art" means that she is always following the ordinariness of beauty around the archive, charting Black women claiming beauty as a space of possibility and life-making.[46] In one moment, Hartman describes a "character" as "know[ing] that beauty was not a luxury, but like food and water, a requirement for living. She loved cashmere sweaters, not because they were expensive, but because the fabric felt so exquisite against her skin, like a thousand fingers caressing her arms, and the cool slip of silk undergarments against her flesh, smooth and releasing all that heat and fire. . . . Beauty and longing provided the essential architecture of her existence. Her genius was exhausted in trying to live."[47] Hartman contends that Black women's demand for beauty in the form of pleasure, excess, and even the ordinary arrangement of a room, flowers in a vase, or rice and vegetables on a plate has been a crucial way that Black women claim autonomy.

This notion of beauty as a practice of Black women's living is echoed by Sharpe's celebration of beauty "as a method," a mode of Black mother-daughter intimacy, and a practice of being together in an anti-Black world. For Sharpe, beauty is a form of remembering her mother and the world she made possible—a refuge and sanctuary from the anti-Black violence that was never far from the window. Sharpe's essay begins with her mother, who, as she tells readers, "gifted me a love of beauty, a love of words. She gave me every black book that was published—and in her practice, birthdays always included gifts for the body, gifts for the mind, and gifts for the soul."[48] It is from these memories of her mother's investments in beauty, words, and "gifts for the soul" that Sharpe asks "what beauty as a method might mean or do: what it might break open, rupture, make possible and impossible. How we might carry beauty's knowledge with us and make new worlds."[49] Beauty is a "Black aesthetic," a Black maternal aesthetic, that births new forms of being. It is also a "Black note," a "telling" or a showing that can "change the course of a life," as when Sharpe's mother urges her to "build a life that [is] nourishing and Black," to "live in spaces where I would be reflected back to myself without particular distortions."[50]

If I think alongside an array of Black feminist work that centers beauty, I am also in conversation with Elaine Scarry's work on beauty as a practice of justice. Scarry insists that when we encounter beauty, we want to replicate it. We want to make a world that makes more beauty possible. She writes, "It makes us draw it, take photographs of it, or describe it to other people. Sometimes it gives rise to exact replication and other times to resemblances, and still other times to things whose connection to the original site of inspiration is unrecognizable."[51] While Scarry's conception of beauty's capacity to unleash justice and empathy, to produce in its viewer a desire to make a different world, is attentive to the work that beauty can make, it is largely uninterested in questions of race and gender. I draw from her writing a sense of beauty's political capacity to make different kinds of worlds. I see her investment in beauty as resonating with Sharpe's provocation that "we might carry beauty's knowledge with us and make new worlds," that beauty is about a turning toward the possible in the midst of temporalities of loss and landscapes of devastation.[52]

There is yet another ethical claim that beautiful writing advances. A Black feminist commitment to the side-by-side-ness of the beautiful and loss takes on great political significance in a moment saturated by scholarly discourses on afropessimism and Black death. What might it mean, contemporary Black feminist theory asks, to approach loss not with an emphasis on Blackness as always the space of death, mourning, and grief? What might it mean to presume that Black women *have* something to lose, rather than that they are subjects who are constituted by having already lost everything, including status as human? I treat beautiful writing's engagement with loss as a critical rejoinder to afropessimism, which presumes the already (social) deadness of Black bodies, *even as this body of work* is often taken up by afropessimist scholars.[53] If afropessimism is a tradition that has centered the impossibility of the Black human—or as Frank Wilderson notes, "Blacks are not Human subjects, but are instead structurally inert props, implements for the execution of White and non-Black fantasies and sadomasochistic pleasures"—it is necessarily in tension with a longer Black feminist tradition that has centered survival, wellness, care, friendship, and intimacy as strategies of safeguarding Black women's bodies and fundamental humanity.[54] My interest is not in casting aside afropessimism—though I do question its investments in theorizing gender and contending with feminism's long, complex, and heterogeneous theoretical and political projects—but instead in suggesting that a contemporary Black feminist theoretical archive, and a commitment to lingering on its strategies of writing beautifully, offers a different way of understanding the relationship between Blackness and loss. When we neglect to consider, to feel *through*, and to engage Black feminist beautiful writing, we fail to see that there are other theoretical traditions that have grappled with the relationship between Blackness and loss. These include both past and more recent Black feminist investments in sitting with and alongside loss without the presumption that Black bodies are themselves only constituted by and through loss.

We

This book insists that there is a we: a cadre of Black feminist theorists who share an aesthetic, ethical, and political commitment to beautiful writing as a method for staying close to loss. This does not mean that the totality of contemporary Black feminist writing is oriented toward the mode of writing I describe here. I am not interested—nor have I ever been—in making a singular claim about a tradition that is vibrantly heterogeneous. And yet I insist that there is a we, that there is a collective project that has taken shape within contemporary Black feminism, and that it is marked by the form of writing and preoccupation with loss that I have described in this chapter.

We has always been a troubling word for feminists. It is an imagined relic of so-called white feminism that Black feminism and women-of-color feminisms are thought to have disrupted—so often Black feminism has problematically been figured merely as disruption—and challenged in their call for heterogeneity, intersectionality, and specificity. In her canonical "Notes toward a Politics of Location," Adrienne Rich asks, "Isn't there a difficulty of saying 'we'? *You cannot speak for me. I cannot speak for us.* Two thoughts:

there is no liberation that only knows how to say 'I'; there is no collective movement that speaks for each of us all the way through. And so even ordinary pronouns become a political problem."[55] Rich's desire for radical specificity as a feminist ethic and her insistence that feminist work requires asking—again and again—"Who are we?" places the question of the challenge (or impossibility) of a collective rooted in the fiction of sameness at the heart of a feminist project. She continues to describe the feminist struggle as one to articulate a "we who are not the same. We who are many and do not want to be the same."[56] Robyn Wiegman also captures the problematic of "we," describing it as "that towering inferno of universalism. That monstrous display of self-infatuation. That master stroke of white-woman-speech . . . But how can I not want this tantalizing hallucination?"[57] Here Wiegman portrays both the intense and long-standing feminist political desire for the "hallucination" of we and the way that desire has long been imagined as a racialized one: the domain of white women.[58]

And yet there is another story about "we" that has emerged in queer-of-color critique, Black feminism, women-of-color feminism, and allied fields. This is one that has coalesced around keywords like *solidarity*, *coalition*, and *dissident friendship*, and that operates around the possibility of a commons rooted in incommensurability (to borrow Joshua Chambers-Letson's formulation).[59] This is a vision of we that thrives without the imagined homogenizing desires of whiteness, the allure and violent trap of sameness. Chambers-Letson describes this vision of the commons as one where "we remain in difference from each other, which is to say that we're not quite one thing but instead a singular being made up of the many, or what Jean-Luc Nancy calls being-singular-plural . . . So rather than the coercive 'we' that dominated the communist parties of historical communism, we became a 'we' in difference from itself."[60] Chambers-Letson's embrace of a "singular-plural" commons, of togetherness in incommensurability, undergirds my investment in a Black feminist "we," one that recognizes rich debate and dissent, the real disagreement at the heart of "we."

To make the argument for a *we*, then, is complicated terrain, especially about a field as varied as Black feminist theory. This book stages a conversation among Black feminist theorists including Tina Campt, Imani Perry, Nicole Fleetwood, Christina Sharpe, Patricia J. Williams, and Saidiya Hartman and Black feminist cultural producers like Elizabeth Alexander, Natasha Trethewey, and Jesmyn Ward, all of whom are engaged in creative public-facing Black feminist work. One of the hallmarks of the *now* is the refusal of Black feminist theory to live or travel apart from either Black women's writing or Black women's intellectual labor. I am not uncritical of the collapse of these terms, even as I understand the political impulse behind insisting that all Black women's intellectual work is social theory. I also understand the claiming of the term *intellectual history* by scholars like Brittney Cooper, Mia Bay, and Farah Jasmine Griffin to be an important political effort to treat Black women's thought not merely as experience, wisdom, or anecdote, but as intellectual production and scholarly labor. As Bay, Griffin, Martha Jones, and Barbara Savage write, "Most scholarship on black women focused on their work as activists, or described them as the objects of intellectual activity, but they rarely received attention as producers of knowledge. What were the intellectual traditions behind black women's activism? How did black women engage with their objectification?"[61] Taken together, this group of writers insists that Black women's writing is intellectual work, that claiming it as an "intellectual tradition" is urgent political labor. Yet Black feminist theory has also long insisted that the academy is not its only audience, or even its primary audience, though it has retained an investment in the university, a space that it denounces as deathly even as we still long for its recognition.[62] This is the paradox at the heart of the move to label Black women's varied cultural production critical theory: it invests in the university as the space that can confer value on Black women's thinking, writing, and producing even as it describes the university as murderous.

My expansive conception of Black feminist theory as including literary and popular-facing work is indebted to how Black feminist theorists have long upended prevailing notions of theory's (or what Barbara Christian might call Theory's) objectivity and neutrality. Black feminist theory has offered a strong challenge to a dominant vision of theory that has moved apart from embodied, spiritual, and experiential modes of knowing and from writing forms that do not prioritize moving their readers. From Christian's insistence that Black people have always "theorized" in forms unrecognizable to the academy to Patricia Hill Collins's plea to recognize the value of an "outsider-within" perspective to Williams's "alchemical" methods as a necessary form of genre-bending, Black feminist theory has repeatedly made the case that doing justice to our objects of study requires not just new forms of thinking but also new forms of writing.[63]

But in the past decade, something has shifted. Black feminism's longstanding commitment to challenging norms of academic writing has become highly visible—even institutionalized—in writing explicitly invested in poiesis, disclosure, proximity to its objects, and intimacy with its reader, including work by Perry, Fleetwood, Campt, Alexander, Sharpe, and Hartman.[64] In many ways, what has changed is that Black feminist theory has made its work as an affective project evident, made clear that Black feminism is, at least in part, a project about feelings—making feelings visible; making clear how feelings are racialized and gendered; thinking about how to feel differently, how to feel better, how to feel anew, how to feel collectively. The body of work that is the subject of this book builds on the pathbreaking work of "theory in the flesh," of anthologies like *This Bridge Called My Back*, *Home Girls*, and *Some of Us Are Brave*, which fused memoir and theory to construct an intimate, multivocal form.[65] As Cherríe L. Moraga and Gloria E. Anzaldúa noted, a theory in the flesh describes "one where the physical realities of our lives—our skin color, the land or concrete we grew up on, our sexual longings—all fuse to create a politic born out of necessity. Here, we attempt to bridge the contradictions in our experience . . . We do this bridging by naming our selves and by telling our stories in our own words."[66] And this archive also builds on work by Audre Lorde (especially her "biomythography" *Zami*) and Alice Walker (especially *In Search of Our Mothers' Gardens*). I name these antecedents to refuse the sense that the *now* is *new* even as I contend that what is different about *now* is how the boundaries between theory and practice, and between scholarly and popular writing, have been profoundly and productively troubled by Black feminist theory, as new markets for Black feminist thought and for Black feminist bodies inside and outside of the academy proliferate. In other words, the intimate voice of Black feminist theoretical writing now has a home—or perhaps homes—in multiple institutions, including the university, the academic press, and the trade press, as well as in a broader academic and cultural imagination that so often turns to Black women's writing as a repository of pain and trauma. This voice has transformed the fields of gender studies and Black studies and has also been taken up in conventional disciplines, even as those fields' relationship to Black feminist theory varies. There are discernible markets and ever-emerging desires for the intimate authorial voice that has come to define Black feminist theoretical innovation, that has come to make Black loss visible and even *feel*-able.

In this book, then, I use the term *Black feminist theory* to describe the writings of a set of authors who primarily work in the university, who primarily publish on academic presses, and who are attached to genealogies of Black feminist theory that are legible in the context of the US university, that circulate across disciplines in the humanities and interpretative social sciences. Even as I do this, I recognize the public and popular reach of many of the works I describe—most notably Hartman's *Wayward Lives*, Sharpe's *In the Wake* and *Ordinary Notes*, and Perry's *Breathe*—and the new visibility of Black feminist academics whose work informs and shapes public conversations about race, gender, and justice.[67] In earlier projects, I considered the popular lives of Black feminist theory alongside intersectionality, tracing the anxiety and defensiveness it has generated as Black feminists watch an analytic that some feel belongs to us move in ways that seem unfamiliar and even jarring. For many Black feminists, this is a source of sadness; for some, it is a source of triumph or an index of institutional power. For me, it is a source of curiosity; I have studied Black feminists' anxious response to Black feminism's circulation—the thing we have desired—more than I have studied the travel of our terms and objects. In other words, I am interested—following Ann duCille's canonical and stunning articulation of Black feminist ambivalence—in what it means to have wanted power, recognition, and legibility; to have fought for it; and now to lament or disavow that very power.[68] In this project I build on that work by considering a moment when Black feminists are in demand and have effectively created a demand for a form of beautiful writing we generated and rendered visible as a method for naming Black loss.

Now

How We Write Now advances a historical claim: that there is a "now," a contemporary body of Black feminist theory that is distinct from earlier iterations of Black feminist theoretical work. To be clear, there is no now that is not indebted to the past. One of the great interventions of Black feminist theory has been its insistence on a palimpsestic conception of time. While I trace a distinction between a *now* and a *then*, I recognize how much the *now* that I think about is indebted to scholars, writers, and cultural producers including Lorde, Anzaldúa, and Walker, key voices that insisted on the experiential and the intimate in feminist writing. So how might we resist the mythology of this moment's exceptionality while grappling with the conditions of the present that are distinct, that produce both a particular Black feminist voice and literary markets for Black women's beautiful writing?

As I trace the contours of now, it is clear that this epoch could be defined in myriad ways: the time of #MeToo, the time of pandemic, the post–Barack Obama years, the Donald Trump years, the post–*Roe v. Wade* years. The texts that are the subject of this book are written in the midst of the Black Lives Matter era, marked by a desire to speak with deep care to the experiences of the "Trayvon Generation," to mobilize tenderness and love in the face of the new hypervisibility and continued persistence of Black death, and in the face of our collective cruel familiarity with witnessing Black death.[69] For Alexander, the "now" is shaped by a newly intimate visibility of Black death. She describes a generation marked by a different kind of closeness with Black death. Images of dead and dying Black bodies are watched on endless loops on small, handheld screens. She writes:

> The kids got shot and the grownups got shot. Which is to say, the kids watched their peers shot down and their parents' generation get gunned down and beat down and terrorized as well. The agglomerating spectacle continues . . . I call the young people who grew up in the past twenty-five years the Trayvon Generation. They always know these stories. These stories framed their world view. These stories helped instruct young African-Americans about their embodiment and their vulnerability. The stories were primers in fear and futility. The stories were the ground soil of their rage. These stories instructed them that anti-black hatred and violence were never far.[70]

Now is marked not just by a proximity to loss but by a feeling of depression, of profound vulnerability; this is an era marked by the new visibility of a collectively held Black grief.

But if this book traces a now marked by the spectacular and intimate visibility of anti-Black violence, this is also a now marked by new markets for Black writing generally, and Black feminist writing particularly. The year 2020 was one of anti-racist reading. As the US became newly attuned to the twin pandemics of anti-Blackness and COVID-19, booksellers and media described the skyrocketing demand for books about race, racism, and remedying the (white) self. In June 2020 the *New York Times* reported that anti-racist books had come to dominate the bestseller lists and quoted Kelly Estep, one owner of Carmichael's Bookstore, who said, "People want these books in hand today. They feel like it's something they can do right now."[71] A year later, the *New York Times* detailed a "crowded field" of books on race and racism across genres from memoir to history, from children's books to short stories.[72] Reading was posited as a way of transforming the self, and anti-racist reading (or, perhaps more accurately stated, anti-racist book buying) was a sign of political solidarity with the demands of Black Lives Matter. As Lauren Michele Jackson noted in her analysis of the proliferation of anti-racist reading lists in 2020, "It's that time again. Race is happening. Never mind that race is always happening but it is *especially* happening now, urgently happening, and god help you if you're not paying attention (though history will probably pardon your procrastination for history, too, is belated). . . . The weeks and months following the 2016 presidential election was such a moment. The *how could this happen* meets the *I told you so.* They rendezvous at the anti-racist reading list."[73] The anti-racist reading list relies on Black women's intellectual labor and depends on the voice and style that Black feminists have honed.

This is a *now* where there is a demand for Black writing—and Black feminist writing—that thinks seriously about how anti-Black violence shapes Black life, particularly Black women's lives. This is a now where Black feminist writers regularly publish in mainstream media to analyze the conditions of the present, to train a broad public to understand the depths of Black loss. This archive includes Rankine's "'The Condition of Black Life Is One of Mourning,'" which I described earlier. Rankine's essay diagnoses Black life as marked by the grief epitomized by Mamie Till Mobley, Emmett Till's mother, whose picture was included in the article as an illustration of the depths of Black maternal loss. This archive also includes Dani McClain's "As a Black Mother, My Parenting Is Always Political," which reminds readers:

> Because of this history, black women have had to inhabit a different understanding of motherhood in order to navigate American life . . . In recent years, this has become especially evident, as dozens of black women and men have had to stand before television cameras reminding the world that their recently slain children were in fact human beings, were loved and sources of joy. The mothers of those killed by police or vigilante violence embody every black mother's deepest fears: that we will not be able to adequately protect our children from or prepare them for a world that has to be convinced of their worth.

I sit with these examples because both are written by Black feminist thinkers, writers, scholars, whose work travels in popular outlets—the *New York Times* and the *Nation* respectively—in the long Black Lives Matter moment, which is not simply attentive to the ongoing conditions that render Black life precarious but also *produces* new literary and journalistic markets to name those conditions. I also mark again the centrality of mothering to this *now*, the fundamental role of Black mothers in making visible, and even embodying, Black loss.

Speaking to public*s* has always been Black feminism's domain, perhaps even more so now in a moment when the demand for writing by and about Black women is thought to offer an urgent response to the conditions of the present.[74] Black feminists have found themselves newly marketable and again reckoning with what it means to find ourselves, as Williams described, "simultaneously universal, trendy, and marginal."[75] If I study the *how* of Black feminist writing, I also always want to think about the markets that have made both possible and profitable an intimate Black feminist voice, one that speaks theory in the vernacular of the experiential. How might we understand a now where Black feminists still continue to decry their marginalization and have accrued significant power and visibility? Perhaps this is a now that duCille helped us anticipate and consider in her brilliant articulation of ambivalence, her studied consideration of the "occultic commodification" that she felt had come to mark the field of Black feminist studies. What does it mean to be desired? And to have *wanted* to be desired? What happens when you get what you want? This is the now that we inhabit—a new iteration of "occultic commodification" that I would describe as the recognition and production of new markets of Black women's beautiful writing that centers loss.

Living With

How We Write Now contends that contemporary Black feminist theory distinctly positions itself as a companion to its readers, offering a map for living with and in loss. Black feminist theory, then, accompanies its readers and becomes far more than a theoretical project and a set of tools for decoding the social world. It becomes a mode of living and feeling, dreaming and being, a distinctly affective project.

The Black feminist theoretical work that I study here positions itself as more than writing, perhaps because writing is figured as far more than words on the page. Maybe this is something that distinguishes Black feminist theory from many other theoretical traditions, the insistence that theory can also be "sacred words."[76] It has become unsurprising to hear Black feminist scholars describe their work as a calling, as soul-work. Even as Black feminists actively name—and bemoan—the labor extracted from Black women in the contemporary university, the actual task of theorizing, of writing, of reading, is so often portrayed not as labor but as something else, something deeply fulfilling, something that moves its practitioners. At times, I have been critical of this insistence on Black feminist theory as life-work—so much of my work has revolved around dislodging what I have seen as romances around Black women, Black women's intellectual production, and Black feminism. I have been wary of the insistence on our own distinctiveness, and critical of the idea that Black feminist intellectual production is—must be—both intellectually rigorous and life-affirming.

But here again my sense of the experiential and of the critical are at odds. I know that I live with Black feminist texts, and this living-with has provided me with a kind of shelter, particularly in this part of my life, where I travel with loss and its seemingly endless duration. I don't know if this living-with Black feminist theory is different from how scholars in other disciplines engage with their theoretical frameworks. I find myself uninterested in a larger claim to Black feminism's singular capacity to change lives, and suspicious of a narrative where Black feminists insist on our importance by emphasizing that Black women are life-saving. But I do know that Black feminist texts have been a companion to me. *Living-with* is about an ethic of companionship that I think animates the Black feminist archive. These are texts that insist there is no distance between writer and object. The authors of the texts I write about do not separate themselves from what they study; they simply cannot. They insist that writing loss requires getting as close to it as possible, refusing or even surrendering distance precisely because the writer is already constituted by loss. They demand that their readers travel with them to inhabit the topography of loss. And they insist that this traveling together— this committed companionship—is a way of doing justice to loss by giving it attention and care rather than running from it.

This book endeavors to ask what it means for Black feminists to live so close to what we write, to be willing to risk so much for what we write. I think about this question differently from many other scholars working in the field of Black feminist theory who track the too-early deaths of Black feminist scholars. Grace Hong, for example, notes, "So many of the black feminists of Christian's generation have died—struck down by cancer and other diseases—including Christian herself in 2000. June Jordan in 2002, Sherley Anne Williams in 1999. Audre Lorde in 1991. Beverly Robinson in 2002. Endesha Ida Mae Holland in 2006. Claudia Tate in 2002. Nellie McKay in 2006. Veve Clark in 2007. In naming these women, these Black feminists, I respond to James Baldwin's imperative to 'bring out your dead.'"⁷⁷ For Hong, the life-energy—intellectual and affective—extracted from Black women scholars is evidence of the violence of the university. As Hong continues, "Bringing out your dead" is a form of Black feminist insistence that "these deaths are systemic, structural. To bring out your dead is not a memorial, but a challenge, not an act of grief, but of defiance, not a register of mortality and decline, but of the possibility of struggle and survival."⁷⁸ And writing this in the weeks after bell hooks's (too-early) death, I am struck by the urgency of "bringing out our dead" and honoring their sacred creative and intellectual work. For Hong, and for other Black feminist and women-of-color feminist scholars, "bringing out your dead" marks the ways that Black feminists' intellectual work and conscription into administrative labor—often in the name of diversity—can be deadly. But I want to consider the question of proximity to our objects differently, as a method and a mode of Black feminist analysis, not just as a death sentence.

This book also aspires to ask another set of questions about *living-with*. I explore how the beautiful voice that I write about here can be mobilized anew to live with loss differently. I ask: How can Black feminism begin to offer accounts of slow loss, of ordinary loss, of loss that is lived and felt in the spaces of the ordinary? How might Black feminism theorize, represent, and describe forms of loss that are nonspectacular, durational, embedded in the conditions of daily life? What might it mean for us to think these losses as Black ones, and thus to think loss at its most capacious, refusing the sense that Black death is only *truly* Black if it can be mobilized as a sign of disparity, anti-Black state violence, or institutionalized neglect? How do I satisfy my own desires for Black feminist beautiful writing that can think about losses of multiple forms, including the quiet ones, forms of loss that are often so hard to write about precisely because we don't know where they begin (and when, if ever, they end)?

My mother's story starts with occasional confusions: a bowl jammed into a toaster oven, dinner plates scrubbed with laundry detergent. Or perhaps the story starts before I knew it started: with a job that used to make her cry and an abrupt decision to quit, a choice that was voiced in the name of "knowing what I want" and "not letting anyone own me." She vowed that she would find *something else*. This *something else* would have an easier commute, a friendlier staff; she would forgo the bus and the subway for a short car ride. This *something else* was the promise of ease. It came at a time when my parents had launched me—I had moved to Washington, DC, and had begun to make the professional life that had been delayed by graduate school for most of my twenties. I can't help but think that my mother felt one portion of her Black maternal labor was complete. She had a few interviews, and then there was silence. Or maybe, if I think about it, the story starts decades before, when I was a little older than my daughter is now. I discovered my mother didn't know how to use an ATM—we called them MAC machines then—and that she was filled with anxiety about the prospect of inserting her card into this machine, entering a code she couldn't remember, and waiting for bills to be spit out at her. Maybe it begins with my long-standing sense, even as a child, that my mother had oriented herself away from life, that my father was acting as her guide, until we reached a moment when he quite literally plays that role, interpreting the world for my mother.

This book maps my desire for the theoretical tradition that has been my intellectual home to offer me tools for living with this slow loss, a loss that, when I begin to write about it, exceeds the frames I have to contain or capture it. As I narrate my mother's story in this book, I am acutely aware that there are portions that feel hard to tell—after all, I miss her terribly even when we sit in the same room—and portions that I cannot tell because I reach the limits of my own knowing. But these are the places where I want Black feminism to live, the places I want Black feminism to help me live with, even as this inhabitation can feel uneasy and uncomfortable.

And there is a final meaning to *living-with*, which feels unbearable to write but crucial to acknowledge as this book is, for me, born from my own experiences of still-unfolding loss. The sense of the seemingly endless duration of Alzheimer's means that I do not know if we are at the beginning of it, in the long middle, or close to the cruel end. We simply find ourselves in this territory, sitting with a loss that is both already here and anticipated, present tense and future tense, the here-and-now and the what-will-come. We live with it, and in it, even as I often tell myself, *Remember, these are the good days*. Slow loss works on time in curious ways that this book endeavors to explore. There is the *now* of the voice that I describe here, the nonlinear deterioration of my mother's brain, the *what might be* time of my mother's future and my own, and my sense of the need to rush this sentence even as I type it: I want her to see this book, even as I already know she will not be able to read it. Yesterday she reads me a text message a friend has sent her. I realize—for the first time—that she now sounds long words out slowly, much as my seven-year-old daughter does. They sit together, breaking down multisyllabic words into short sounds my mother can pronounce. *Make your mouth into an o*, my daughter advises. I am moved by the tenderness of this scene. I am destroyed by the tragedy of it too. It is this feeling of being moved and destroyed in the scene of ordinary loss, and the Black feminist attempt to do justice to it with beautiful language, that constitutes the heart of this book.

2

Staying at the Bone

If you can stay at the bone of what's true, then that's your lifeboat.

ELIZABETH ALEXANDER

When I pick up Elizabeth Alexander's memoir *The Light of the World*, I think of my mother.

For much of my life, my mother was a reader. For much of my life, my mother was also a commuter. In 1972, when my mother was a sophomore at Vassar College, her roommate—a young woman my mother found to be almost unbearably cool—offered her a ride home to New York City for Thanksgiving break. My grandfather—whom my mother found to be unbearably uncool—felt it was unsafe for a relatively inexperienced driver to brave the roads when an ice storm was predicted. He told my mother he would drive to Poughkeepsie, New York, the next morning to pick her up. My mother fell asleep in anger and woke up to a knock at her door and the news that her roommate had died in a car accident. In the wake of her dear friend's death, my mother decided she would never drive. This was a manageable decision when she lived in New York City, but less so when my parents moved to New Jersey seeking a space of their own.

For many of my earliest days, my mother made our lengthy walking expeditions into adventures. We would collect acorns and red-tinged autumn leaves; we would describe everything we observed on our walks. But we lived in the commuter suburbs of northern New Jersey, and little was set up for walking. We were oddities. Friends would tell us that they saw us—"I spotted you on Cedar Lane," or "I saw you carrying groceries home from the store." We walked with grocery bags, with library books, with take-out pizza boxes. We walked and walked until it became untenable—my mother would pick me up from preschool, and as the summer evenings yielded to cooler fall nights, we walked home in darkness. It was this darkness that convinced my mother to learn how to drive.

She was thirty when she failed her first driving test. I can still remember standing in the rain in my ugly green raincoat, watching my mother efficiently drive the front tire of her car over an orange cone. I wasn't certain what the orange cone was supposed to mark, but I was certain that it didn't belong under the wheel of our car. I remember a silent ride back to my parents' house. And I can remember that my mother cried uncontrollably, that she stomped her feet on the dining room floor and later announced that she needed a "real driving teacher," thus ending her prolonged and contentious weekend driving lessons with my father, and my weekends spent slumped in the back seat of a car reading *Ramona Quimby*. My mother hired a young man in his early twenties with a thick swoop of hair and a sense of humor, and she learned to drive.

Six months later, when she had finally secured her license, she bought a small blue Honda. It had manual windows and a large ashtray that she would fill with cigarette butts. I knew even at my young age that the car was about a certain kind of freedom that she felt she had achieved, one that she wanted to celebrate. And even though she refused to take it on the highway, preferring what she called "side streets," navigating from place to place slowly on quiet roads, she would still slide the radio knob to the end of the dial—107.5—and turn on her favorite slow jams and sing and smoke and drive. Sometimes her best friend from Vassar, Mary, would come. Mary would drink from a two-liter bottle of Diet Coke while my mother drove and they exchanged stories about people I didn't know. This might be the freest—the most unencumbered—I ever saw her.

But even though she was a newly minted driver with her own car, the easiest way to get from my parents' house to my mother's job in Brooklyn was on public transportation. And so, for much of my life, my mother was a commuter. She would take the bus to the Port Authority and then two subways to her office. She would come home at the end of the day with a metallic smell: the odor of trains and buses and the sheer effort required to push one's body through so many spaces and then come home. She would eat and rest and then do it again. She would make her trip with the company of a book and the weekly *New York Times Magazine*, which she would roll tightly into a compact cylinder. My mother relished that time between work and the relentless demands of a still-young child. It was a time she could spend in the company of her imagination.

This portion of our story feels harder to write. It is an attempt to describe a moment—one of many—when I suspected things were unraveling but wasn't quite sure why or what or how. These were the moments when my husband and I would exchange a perplexed stare but would maintain our faith in confusion or accident, our shared hope that things would get better. But in retrospect, this is a story of the beginning—or maybe the middle—of the moment we find ourselves in now.

Seven years ago, my husband and I spent a week with my parents on a beach vacation, except my parents aren't really ones for the beach—or perhaps they like the idea of the beach more than the beach itself. One day, we managed to get them to bring their chairs to the shore with us. My mother brought two objects with her, her perfectly rolled-up copy of the *New York Times Magazine*—which she had folded as if she was going to read it on a crowded subway car—and Alexander's *The Light of the World*.

Stay at the bone, Alexander emphasizes. And that's what I'm trying to do here.

My mother carried *The Light of the World* with her for much of that summer. She would read a sentence or two and stop. She would sigh. She would open the book again, never turning a page. She would read a few sentences and close the book. But one day the book vanished. *How was it?* I asked. *Intense*, she said. *I'm still coming down from it.*

This was a period in her life when my mother began using the word *intense* with regularity: to describe a slice of pecan pie, a Sunday crossword puzzle, the blast of air-conditioning in a restaurant, the light fixture in my parents' living room, *The Light of the World*. I didn't know how to understand her use of this word, which always came with annoyance, with a sense of having been intruded on. It was as if the world was inflicting itself on her, as if she was marking her attention to the ferocity of what I found to be the most seemingly ordinary parts of living. In retrospect, I understand her to be describing a new place and a sense that the conditions of everyday life—as they had unfolded for years without remark—were simply too much.

I used to understand the intensity of *The Light of the World* that my mother was describing to be her encounter with the book's intimate exploration of the contours of grief. But now I understand it differently. I realize that this was the beginning of my mother losing her capacity to read. It's not that she couldn't read then, or that she can't now. It's that she can no longer guarantee that when she reaches the end of a sentence, she'll remember what was at the beginning. This makes reading onerous, or wholly impossible. My mother has forgotten so many words now; when she wants something, she'll often describe what work the object performs. A fork has become *the thing you hold in your hand to eat*. A menu has become *the list of food*. A bathroom has become *the place you go*.

Seven years after the summer spent in the company of Alexander's book and my mother's forgetting, I write the beginning words of this chapter. We are on vacation with my parents, and I approach it with a keen sense that I'm not sure if my mother will be able to travel again. She is happy to be here, but she isn't sure where here is. After our first dinner together, she hands me a box of leftovers and tells me to take it home with me. I say, "Mom, I'm staying here with you." She seems excited to hear this, even though hours before she saw me emptying my car of suitcases. Everything feels deeply present tense—because this very moment will quickly be forgotten—and like something that I should tightly hold on to because everything that is to come will be harder than this. It is also the case that my mother is changing before my eyes, that a softness that used to be—or so I thought—fundamental to her personality has been replaced by something else, an edginess, a perpetual sense of frustration. I want to spend time with her; I find it hard to spend time with her; I feel guilty about finding it hard. This cycle repeats.

My mother keeps a copy of Stacey Abrams's *Our Time Is Now* on her night table. I have no idea where it came from, but I am certain that her persistent loyalty to buying books by Black women authors led her to this purchase. Some old loyalties persist, including this one, even when her capacity to read the book she has purchased is gone. She opens the book again and again and then closes it. She remembers that she was a reader, and she can't bear to surrender that identity, even though there is no way she can read this book now. And so the book sits there, a reminder of something she used to do, someone she used to be. There is something moving about this to me, about her fierce attachment to aspects of an earlier identity that simply cannot be shed. I am also moved by what I see as her desire to enact something for me, and for my daughter, to assure us that everything is just fine, that she is who she always was. My daughter whispers, "Grandma is reading a book. I think things are getting better." "Yes," I tell her, "yes, this is a good sign." I tell her this because sometimes I can't bear to name the cruel truth of the place we find ourselves in.

For me, the story of losing my mother begins, at least in part, with *The Light of the World*. If I am to stay close to the bone, I have to sit with that book, not as a metaphor for loss, but as a physical object where my narration—or *one* narration—of losing her begins.

In 2017 Sheryl Sandberg and Elizabeth Alexander were featured in a *New York Times* conversation titled "On Love, Loss and What Comes Next." Sandberg and Alexander had both published memoirs in the aftermath of losing their husbands. Alexander describes the centrality of her writing practice to navigating loss: "I was surprised that so shortly after my husband passed, maybe two weeks later, I started writing things down. It felt unseemly, almost cannibalistic. It was the only way I could know what was happening to me. I knew I was alive; I knew I had to take care of my children. But writing was like placing my hand on the earth. It wasn't comfortable. It was more like living with the steady companion of my life: making things out of experience."[1] For Alexander, writing is a practice of proximity, a way of staying close to both love and loss. In the opening page of her memoir, she writes, "The story seems to begin with catastrophe but in fact began earlier and is not a tragedy but rather a love story. Perhaps tragedies are only tragedies in the presence of love, which confers meaning to loss. Loss is not felt in the absence of love. 'The queen died and then the king died' is a plot, wrote E. M. Forster in *The Art of the Novel*, but 'The queen died and then the king died of grief' is a story."[2] Alexander's starting point—that the presence of loss is evidence of the existence of love—is one of the claims that contemporary Black feminist writing stages in favor of living *with* loss rather than trying to outlive loss. While I think loss makes visible—sometimes uncomfortably—a host of other feelings beyond love (including ambivalence), I travel with her idea that staying close to loss tells us something about intensity, attachment, and even the myth-making that can accompany loss.

Stay at the bone.
Place a hand on the earth.
Live with the steady companion.

A set of pleas that insist not just that writing practice a proximity to loss but also that we surrender metaphor and insist on materiality, that we stay close to matter, that we act as witnesses of the granular, the small detail, the quiet gesture. If in the previous chapter I offered a description of the preoccupations of beautiful Black feminist writing, staying at the bone unites these efforts. Staying at the bone is a commitment not simply to sitting with loss but to attending to its material details: What does loss *look* like? What does it *feel* like? How does it make its presence known? How might we describe it through a practice of slow and sustained attention?

This chapter takes as its central object contemporary Black feminist writing that treats staying at the bone as a strategy for living with loss, for getting close to it. The texts that I study resist escaping or moving away from loss; they also refuse to think what comes "after" loss. There is no after, they insist, even as each text is situated differently vis-à-vis the scene of loss. Alexander continues, "My husband's death ravaged me, but it's meant to. If we have any life span, we don't outrun this stuff. It may not be a husband at 47 or 50, but these things will happen. Somehow, we have to let the ravages shape us and make our souls stronger and more beautiful. Because that is life."[3] I study how "let[ting] the ravages shape us" takes on a written form for Black feminist theorists, and how the voice that emerges from the "ravages" is one that moves with radical specificity, with a kind of deeply vulnerable attention to the scene of loss and its textures and sensations.

The call to stay at the bone is deeply resonant with other feminist advocacy for specificity as an ethic, including Adrienne Rich's canonical "Notes toward a Politics of Location." Rich calls for a

> moratorium on saying "the body." For it's also possible to abstract "the" body. When I write "the body" I see nothing in particular. To write "my body" plunges me into lived experience, particularity: I see scars, disfigurements, discolorations, damages, losses, as well as what pleases me. Bones well-nourished from the placenta; the teeth of a middle-class person seen by the dentist twice a year from childhood. White skin, marked and scarred by three pregnancies, an elected sterilization, progressive arthritis, four joint operations, calcium deposits, no rapes, no abortions, long hours at a typewriter—my own, not in a typing pool—and so forth. To say "the body" lifts me away from what has given me a primary perspective. To say "my body" reduces the temptation to grandiose assertions.[4]

Not *the* body, *my* body.

No space for abstraction or distance.

For Rich, radical specificity is about recognizing that knowledge comes from the place—the literal space—in and from which we speak. Rich's politics of location is a complicated affair, one that sees Black feminist writers as performing (and maybe embodying) the politics of location she wants to enact. Yet I draw from her an interest in speaking from one's own body, as a location and as a politics. For the Black feminist writers that I take up, specificity is about an attempt to provide both loss and those who have been lost with companionship. It is also, perhaps paradoxically, an attempt to contend with the failures of language to capture loss's excess through an attention to detail. We can never represent the immensity and specificity of loss, but we can describe the smell of a hospital, the worn covers of magazines on a doctor's waiting room table, the rough fabric of a blood pressure cuff.

As I argue throughout this book, proximity offers the promise of getting a handle on loss, wrapping one's arms around it, describing its contours with a kind of certainty. Yet loss always exceeds language and refuses our attempts to fix it. Its capacity to shape-shift means that it challenges any discursive effort to capture it. The texts that are the subject of this chapter grapple with this conundrum—the idea that living with loss is practiced through writing that stays at the bone *and* the idea that staying at the bone is itself a kind of fiction, a practice that can be both fulfilling and incomplete simultaneously. Staying at the bone relies on memory and archives, both of which are seductive and imperfect, both of which offer clarity and opacity simultaneously. Writing that stays at the bone always brushes up against the limits of what can be known and named, even if it might not name—or recognize—those limits. What's more: it is not possible to *always* be at the bone, to *stay* there: It is exhausting. It is relentless. It is a form of exposure that can feel both exhilarating and devastating. It is a form of vulnerability that perhaps cannot be inhabited for the duration of a text, or that can only be partially inhabited, or that wears at its writer even as its writer insists on staying there.

The writing that is the subject of this chapter—Jesmyn Ward's "Witness and Respair" (2020), Elizabeth Alexander's *The Light of the World* (2015), and Natasha Trethewey's *Memorial Drive* (2020)—makes the argument that staying at the bone is the central Black feminist mode of living with loss. The losses that they "stay" with are intimate and sudden ones: two focus on the loss of a beloved, and the labor and duty of continuing to mother in the face of grief;

the third centers on the loss of a mother. They also each offer distinct interpretations on the plea to stay with the material: Ward's essay thinks about staying at the bone as a practice of witnessing. Alexander's memoir makes the claim that dream, chance, and fate also have a materiality—and a Black materiality—that must be written to narrate her loss. Trethewey's memoir grapples with the materiality of evidence as she assembles an archive of her mother's murder. She contends with how to "stay at the bone" in the face of multiple forms of official evidence that offer their own account of violence, death, and loss. The texts collectively reveal that "the bone" is a complicated place—and sometimes staying there paradoxically requires moving to the metaphorical, ethereal, or abstract.

Respair

An antiquated word. That's what catches my eye about Jesmyn Ward's essay "Witness and Respair," published in *Vanity Fair*. Nancy Friedman writes, "You'd think that such an interesting and useful word would have a long and vigorous life in the language. But instead *respair* languished—at least until March 2017, when Lane Greene . . . included it in an essay about why words die. As a noun, *respair* means 'the return of hope after a period of despair.'"[5] Ward's essay was published in the long moment in 2020 when we were ordered to "socially distance" (except those marked as "essential workers," overwhelmingly people of color, who were compelled to risk their lives and continue working outside of the household) and when the pandemic reoriented our ordinary lives in familiar and painful raced, classed, and gendered forms. Her essay was also published after George Floyd's murder on a Minneapolis street in May 2020 captivated national attention and produced a national "reckoning" with anti-Blackness that took its most public form in a summer of widely circulating statements crafted by corporations, institutions, and universities, often accompanied by reading lists that promised consumers that they could read their way into an anti-racist self, transform themselves through an encounter with words. A word like *respair* had particular appeal in the early days of the pandemic, when many of us desperately looked for a way forward in a time that offered no promise of ending. For Ward, respair is the landscape that opened up in the curious intersection of her Beloved's sudden and unexpected death and the transformation of the world by the demands of Black Lives Matter. Ward's brief essay traverses the complicated landscape of grief as both deeply personal and collective: it stays at the bone of private and national loss and insists that intimate loss is also shared.

Ward's essay begins with a description of a seemingly ordinary illness that strikes her family. She and her children are diagnosed with the flu, and her husband's tests are inconclusive. Ward and her children quickly recover, but her husband remains sick. She writes:

> Two days after our family doctor visit, I walked into my son's room where my Beloved lay, and he panted: *Can't. Breathe.* I brought him to the emergency room, where after an hour in the waiting room, he was sedated and put on a ventilator. His organs failed: first his kidneys, then his liver. He had a massive infection in his lungs, developed sepsis, and in the end, his great strong heart could no longer support a body that had turned on him. He coded eight times. I witnessed the doctors perform CPR and bring him back four. Within 15 hours of walking into the emergency room of that hospital, he was dead. The official reason: acute respiratory distress syndrome. He was 33 years old.[6]

Loss: sudden and unexpected. Ward narrates this loss through the words that became the rallying cry of Black Lives Matter: *I can't breathe.* The words became a way of honoring Floyd, a strategy for marking how anti-Blackness operates by stamping out Black breath, and a way of naming a wish for Black life. But in Ward's essay, those same words mark her Beloved's final days on earth, the moments before his "great strong heart could no longer support a body that had turned on him." The signifiers of the pandemic—ventilators, respiratory failure, emergency rooms—become, for Ward, the signs of unexpected personal tragedy.

What does it mean to experience loss during a time of seemingly endless loss? Ward describes this as an awareness that her "loss was a tender second skin," that it was incorporated into her body, that it *became* part of her.[7] Evidence of loss is everywhere, in every fold and corner of ordinary life, as she describes: "The absence of my Beloved echoed in every room of our house. Him folding me and the children in his arms on our monstrous fake-suede sofa. Him shredding chicken for enchiladas in the kitchen. Him holding our daughter by the hands and pulling her upwards, higher and higher, so she floated at the top of her leap in a long bed-jumping marathon. Him shaving the walls of the children's playroom with a sander after an internet recipe for homemade chalkboard paint went wrong: green dust everywhere."[8] Every space signals her Beloved's absence: the house is forever changed, transformed into a repository for the endless "echoes" of grief. And the house is also forever changed because of the pandemic, because her children are suddenly home-schooled, because the world has halted, because her children "cried hysterically . . ." and at the same time, "there was no bleach, no toilet paper, no paper towels for purchase anywhere."[9] The world was coming undone and undone and undone again, grief spilling into what she calls "hot, wordless grief."

Perhaps what Ward's essay does most profoundly is to make a case for attention as a practice of love, for staying at the bone as a mode of care. Ward calls this practice of staying at the bone *witnessing*, and it is a practice that connects her personal grief to the feeling of respair she felt in the midst of the racial reckoning—to use the word of the day—that followed Floyd's murder. What unites these losses, and the grief that swirled around them, is a sense of what witnessing opens up and makes possible. As her Beloved was dying, Ward insisted on staying close to him, performing what she describes as showing that "*we ain't going nowhere.*" She narrates this through recounting the sounds and images of standing next to someone as they die. Ward reminds her readers of what a doctor told her as her Beloved was dying: "The last sense to go is hearing. When someone is dying, they lose sight and smell and taste and touch. They even forget who they are. But in the end, they hear you."[10] And so Ward tells us—her readers—what she heard: "the prayer that dissolves midair," "the hush-click-hush-click of the ventilator drowns it."[11] This willingness to have been there, to have seen it and remembered it, constitutes a sacred and "terrible commitment" to her Beloved. To stand over someone who can't breathe, to manifest this "terrible" and tender commitment, is, Ward insists, a form of love forged in the face of grief. To continue to remember and to witness is also an enduring form of love and a practice of living with loss.

Ward's unexpected loss ruptures the paradigm of Black loss that expects and anticipates sudden death in the form of anti-Black violence but not in the form of undiagnosed respiratory distress. But witnessing, Ward insists, is also about connecting her intimate loss to the larger landscape of loss that marked pandemic-time and the demands of Black Lives Matter in 2020. She seeks to connect these losses, revealing that staying close to the bone is also about recognizing shared losses, bearing witness to connections among experiences of grief. She published her essay a few months after the pandemic began, in a moment where witnessing was complex terrain. While Floyd's murder was captured on cameras and played and replayed on televisions, computer screens, and iPhones, those killed by the pandemic largely died off-screen. The iconography of the pandemic consisted of images of the president, frontline workers, and visuals of economic crisis, not of the staggering numbers of those who died. In May 2020, Sarah Elizabeth Lewis offered a poignant critique of the invisibility of pandemic deaths, insisting that "for society to respond in ways commensurate with the importance of this pandemic, we have to see it. For us to be transformed by it, it has to penetrate our hearts as well as our minds. Images force us to contend with the unspeakable. They help humanize clinical statistics, to make them comprehensible. They step into the breach."[12] (That same month, the *New York Times'* front page listed the names of the nearly 100,000 people who had died from COVID in the US by the end of May 2020, declaring it an "incalculable loss.")[13] Ward's essay asks what it means to feel intimate loss in a moment when the nation is radically transformed by collective grief, and even by experiences of grief that could not be collectively mourned because of the mandate to stay physically separate and because of a national preoccupation with *not* seeing the dead, a preoccupation that persists as we talk about the "post-pandemic" era even as the pandemic continues.

She contends with what it means to stand as a witness to her Beloved's death, as a witness to Floyd's murder, and as a witness to a radical social upheaval that promised—at least momentarily—that things could be different. She asks us—her readers—to consider how we have all become witnesses of various sorts, particularly as news outlets played and replayed the video of Floyd's murder, and how that witnessing has transformed us.[14] Of course, sometimes media make us only into spectators in their endless displaying of images of Black death. And for Ward the spectator and the witness are categorically different subject positions, with the witness acting as a companion and incorporating that loss into their sense of self. In an interview published in the wake of Floyd's murder, Elizabeth Alexander notes, "To the question of who's watching, what happens when black people watch? To inform is one thing, to bear witness is another thing. But to just roll the video without a moment that says a life was taken here, a person was dehumanized here in the way that black people have been dehumanized throughout our history? Seeing is important, and helps you understand. But I think the repetition of that image without thought to who's watching it and how it affects them is something that we could work on a little bit."[15] Alexander, like Ward, explicates that witnessing and watching are different, that being a spectator and a witness are qualitatively and ethically distinct positions. What Ward shows is that witnessing is a mode of being with and a practice of care. It is a form of staying close to the bone, a practice that can connect intimate losses and collective losses.

In the haze of her own loss, her sense of the everyday remade, Ward describes watching Black Lives Matter protests on television. What she felt was that Black loss was finally being witnessed, that Black pain was collectively seen. As she notes, "The revelation that Black Americans were not alone in this, that others around the world believed that Black Lives Matter broke something in me, some immutable belief I'd carried with me my whole life."[16] The landscape of loss, she argues, can open up the power and possibility of witnessing, the "terrible commitment" to see trauma and pain and to respond with love and solidarity. I concede that it is hard to read Ward's words now—four years later—without a sense that her optimism about the possibility of transformation was misguided. If she felt that "Black Americans were not alone in this," that the world had changed, it now feels increasingly—again—like Black Americans *are*, in fact, alone in this. The promise of a racial "reckoning" in 2020 gave way to endless diversity, equity, and inclusion (DEI) initiatives, neologisms, and anti-racist bureaucracies that proved to be more of a public relations stunt than a meaningful transformation. But I want to honor a moment when she saw loss release a new territory, one where "droves of people . . . moving like a river down the boulevards" protested and gathered, raged and shouted, and dreamed. I want to hold space for her commitment to witnessing as a radical act of solidarity, a way of being together—even if fleeting—that opened up the space for feeling different, for letting loss stand as a fertile ground for living together and imagining something else. I also want to mark the tender space she opens up for thinking about the intimate connections between personal loss and collective loss, for grieving together—across scales of loss—as a form of getting to the bone together. Ward leaves her readers with the sense that while there is no "after" to loss, there is the possibility of respair, the door that witnessing gently pushes open after a long period of anguish.

Fullness

Elizabeth Alexander's *The Light of the World* (2015) is a rumination on the feeling of fullness. Much of the book describes the act of feeding others—family, friends, community—and the act of being fed as forms of world-making, as practices of holding those we love close. Jeff Gordinier's review of the memoir notes, "If there is a romantic subplot in the book, it's the story of their mutual love for food over their 15-year marriage, of how recipes and rituals of eating animated their time together. Food makes an appearance on seemingly every other page: Italian pastries and espresso in the East Village, figs in a backyard garden, Easter bread baked with hard-boiled eggs."[17] I would describe this "mutual love for food" as about far more than food; it is evidence of a shared desire to feed each other and community, a sense of making a home for each other and others in the world, a combined will to produce the conditions through which people feel a sense of fullness. Alexander's memoir includes a number of recipes for her husband's celebrated dishes she writes about in the book, including his shrimp barka, a dish so famous that "women called for it from St. Raphael and Yale-New Haven Hospital after they'd delivered their babies; people said they literally dreamed of it, a fairy food that tasted like nothing else."[18] But the book's recipes aren't simply to instruct readers in the preparation of decadent meals; they are an account of a rich life, and they give the memoir the feeling of a scrapbook, a prolonged eulogy, a celebration. In that same review, Farah Jasmine Griffin describes Alexander and Ficre Ghebreyesus's house as "a space where they created beautiful things—food and babies and art."[19] A house committed to life. This form of life-making is electric; it is sustaining; it makes possible its own replication with the vitality of the house producing creativity, conversation, time and space to write and to paint. As Alexander notes, "We searched for a table big enough to accommodate feasts of friends and extended family in the dining room I had painted a color I called 'Venetian pink,' for Ficre. We relished our role as Command Central. We would live here but two years as a family of four, and a year and four months and fifteen days as a family of three."[20] The book opens as a celebration of "command central" as a mode of living, of beauty as a practice of offering fulfillment and satiety.

This capacity to be nourished and to nourish others, as Alexander narrates it retrospectively, comes through the intensity of her connection with her husband, Ficre Ghebreyesus. Her life with Ghebreyesus was different, she tells us, even from the very beginning. The arrival of this love can only be narrated in the register of the predestined. This is a different form of staying close to the bone, one that requires an appeal to magic, to destiny, to the cosmic as a mode of explaining the depths of their intimacy. Perhaps this is a kind of staying at the bone that requires romance. (*The Light of the World* is, to be clear, a romance. In perhaps the only unromantic moment in the book,

Alexander notes, "In all marriages there is struggle and ours was no different in that regard. But we always came to the other shore, dusted off, and said, There you are, my love.")[21] Before Alexander meets Ghebreyesus, a psychic tells her, "'You better get yourself together, girl, . . . because your man is on his way and you can't stop this love from coming. This is no regular Negro,' Reggie said. 'He's from someplace tiny that no one's ever heard of.'"[22] The arrival of "no regular Negro," of a love that was "coming" and couldn't stop, becomes central to how Alexander narrates the feeling of being fed: a life this full is made possible by a love that was scripted, that was fated to be "on its way." It is "Reggie-the-Psychic-of-Brooklyn-New-York" who tells her what is to come: a painter, a baby, a full life. A few weeks later, Alexander sits in a café and meets Ghebreyesus and feels what she describes as "a torque inside my stomach, the science of love."[23] Perhaps, she suggests, a love of this magnitude can only be explained through destiny or fate. Perhaps, she reveals, the only way to stay close to the bone is to gesture to the mysteries of the universe that elude fixed description.

The idea of a preordained love is, for Alexander, also an idea of a Black diasporic love. She writes, "When we first became lovers, we entered a three-day, three-night vortex. Night one, I slept Senghor's 'deep Negro sleep' for the first time ever, lifelong insomniac no more."[24] This love that could be explained only through an appeal to the intuitive is one that can change bodies and their rhythms. This is a connection, she insists, that was formed long before she and her beloved were even born, one that was forged between two Black women across the Atlantic. She continues, "The story begins in 1962, where two women in cotton lawn maternity shirts approach the end of their pregnancies, one in Asmara, Eritrea, one in Harlem, USA. The low-hanging moon of impending childbirth governs their days. The ones we may come to love have been born by the time we start longing for them, and so my beloved and I came onto this earth in March and in May of 1962, halfway around the world from each other."[25] Their love takes on an epic quality, a "story" that begins when two Black women "halfway around the world from each other" birthed two children who would become lovers, homemakers, beauty forgers, parents. There is no way to understand the intensity of their love without thinking about Black connections and intimacies across geographies.

But if love is Black, is loss as well? Much of the book takes up this question as Alexander presents Ghebreyesus's death both as deeply intimate *and* as Black loss. This is perhaps one of the great tensions that Alexander's memoir navigates, as she thinks about how grief is both personal (*her* loss) and collective, how Ghebreyesus's too-soon death can be understood only through the frame of racial disparity, a frame that can efface his particularity and singularity. Alexander narrates her husband's death as, at least in part, a Black death. She writes, "One cardiologist I spoke to after his passing says he believes unequivocally that the stress of growing up in war and being a refugee affected his heart."[26] In another moment, she reminds her readers that "Black men die more catastrophically, across class, than anybody else in America . . . He was an African man, an Eritrean man, and an African American man. He was a black man . . . His big heart burst. The autopsy later tells us his arteries were blocked nearly completely."[27] Alexander's insistence on Ghebreyesus's sudden, surprising death as Black loss requires her to remind her readers that he was "an African man, an Eritrean man, and an African American man." In this account her seemingly intimate loss is one that is also about the embodied costs of war, dispossession, and anti-Blackness, about what some scholars have termed *weathering* and the embodied costs of trauma.[28]

But when Alexander sees her husband's body in the hospital after his death, she insists on the intimacy of the loss, on the parts of her husband that are hers and hers alone. Alexander describes seeing her husband's body in the hospital after his death and claiming the intensity and privacy of her loss. She writes:

> The penis, which is mine alone, lies sleeping on his thigh, nestled in its hair, the heart outside his body, and that is what I remember of his body, after the emergency room doctor met my eyes and made his pronouncement. Him, still him, still Ficre, still a him, the last trace of him. The penis with which we actually made the human beings who are our children, is sign and symbol and substance of what I have lost. I lie atop him. And cover his body with my body. After time that cannot be measured someone I do not know comes and puts her arms around my shoulders and gently, gently leads me off and away from Ficre.[29]

Mine alone.

I want to sit with this moment: not merely its refusal of the abstract frame of Black loss but its insistence on the deep intimacy of loss. Alexander describes the penis "sleeping on his thigh," the penis as "sign and symbol and substance," as something that she frames as hers. I want to think of this moment as so deeply close to the bone, as tethering loss to flesh, as treating the penis as "sign and symbol" of *her* loss. This "sign and symbol" is one that Alexander interprets as the "last trace of him" after his death, and as a trace that perhaps only she can identify. Alexander shows brilliantly how loss can be both a story of disparity, forced migration, violence, anti-Blackness, *and* a story of the painfully intimate realization of seeing what is "hers alone" for the last time.

Ultimately, Alexander's memoir is largely concerned with the question of living with loss, with how one feels fed in the presence of loss, with a life that is lived after one is led "off and away from" one's beloved. Because Alexander insists that love indexes loss, living with loss as a companion is a testament to the intensity of love, a kind of commitment. Here I do not mean to romanticize loss and grief, as I do not think that is what Alexander aspires to do. Instead, she presents writing as a process and practice of living-with, a way of staying close to loss and to those who are lost. Writing allows her to grapple with the question of how loss is intimate and social simultaneously, personal and communal. What is lost with her husband's death, she reveals, is their intense bond, and also the fullness of the communal life they had forged. When asked about the process of writing the book, she says, "Part of what was beautiful about writing the book was that I was with him."[30] Loss becomes a territory navigated by writing precisely because writing loss is a practice of staying close to those she holds dearest.

Even still, she is clear that loss changes writing. The portions of her memoir devoted to *living-with*, to the aftermath of loss, showcase a different kind of writing. Her chapters grow shorter; some are just a few sentences. And many are preoccupied with dreams, with precisely the kind of intuitive knowledge that begins the memoir. It is in dreams, Alexander reveals, that she can continue to be close to her husband, that their love lives on. And it is dreaming that allows her to see him, to touch him, to feel herself in physical proximity to him. In one dream she sees a chapel, and then "we left the church and walked hand-in-hand to the corner store. I could feel my hand in his, then as now . . . The light changed. And then he was gone from the dream."[31] Or in another one, she writes, "How powerfully I feel you are somewhere, but not here. You come to me in another dream with a missing tooth and an unfamiliar red jacket; I know every single article of clothing you own, right down to the last sock and undershirt. Do you make friends and have companions where you are?"[32] Here, again, Alexander grapples with the complex territory of intimacy and collectivity, what it means to know "every single article of clothing you own" and to see her beloved wearing something unknown, the shock of unfamiliarity. What might it mean, she asks, to want company for her beloved in a landscape that is unknown to her, one she does not yet occupy—something we might call an afterlife—to hope that he has friends and companions there? The memoir concludes with a dream:

> I dream we are moving, my family of four: Lizzy, Ficre, Solomon, and Simon. It is light and easy . . . At a fork in the road, Ficre lets my hand go and waves me on. You have to keep walking, Lizzy, he says. I know it is the only truth, so I walk. I look back. I look back. I can still see him smiling and waving me on. It was the two of us walking the road and now he has let my hand go. I walk. I can always see him. His size does not change as I move forward: he is five foot nine and a half, exactly right. I can still feel the feel of my hand in his hand as I walk.[33]

But what do we make of the dream and its relationship to the bone? Is this a moment of staying with it or moving away from it, a commitment to the materiality of loss and its capacity to consume even a dream or a need for a reprieve? Perhaps, as when Alexander describes meeting her beloved for the first time, dream, predestination, and imagination have their own materiality that she aspires to give shape to. Perhaps staying at the bone can exceed language—as loss so often does—requiring us to move to other terrains to describe and capture both the immensity of love and the immensity of loss.

Evidence

"The record," Natasha Trethewey writes, "shows murder."[34] *Memorial Drive* begins when Trethewey finds an old photograph of her mother, one that inaugurates Trethewey's attempt to construct her own record of her mother, and that interacts with and challenges the official "record." Indeed, much of the book is a rumination on questions of evidence, archives, and witnessing, and a study of the intersections between juridical records of violence and the records of memory, both of which are faulty. As Trethewey narrates:

> When I finally sit down to write the part of our story I've most needed to avoid, when I force myself at last to read the evidence, all of it—the transcripts, witness accounts, the autopsy and official reports, the ADA's statement, indications of police indifference—I collapse on the floor, keening as though I had just learned of my mother's death.

What comes out is uncontrollable: the long, unbroken, primal wailing I never allowed myself back then. So I live it again in real time, only what I am reliving now is not my own feeling of sudden loss, but rather the terror of her last moments.[35]

What is the relationship between staying close to the bone, to "our story," and the records that attempt to capture that story? How does one stay close to the bone given the faultiness of all kinds of archives? And what happens when the memories of loss are contained—at least partially—in juridical archives, in case files, in homicide reports, in crime scene photographs? How do those official archives interact with one's private archive of grief?

Trethewey's memoir begins with a description of a formal portrait that her mother had taken a few months before her death. It is the last image of her mother that lives on, aside from photographs taken of her mother at the crime scene. Her mother is forty years old in the picture, and Trethewey reports that "she does not look at the camera, her eyes fixed at a point in the distance that seems to be just above my head, making her face as inscrutable as it always was."[36] Trethewey understands the image as one that was taken out of a desire "to document herself as woman come this far, the rest of her life ahead of her."[37] It is full of anticipation and promise, a celebration that she had "come this far" and excitement at what was ahead. But Trethewey also realizes that "hindsight makes me see the portrait differently now— how gloomy it is. . . . [S]omething else is there, elegiac even then: a strange corner of light just behind her head, perhaps the photographer's mistake, appearing as though a doorway has opened, a passage through which, turning, she might soon depart."[38] The photograph enters the book as a kind of evidence. It is at once a record of anticipation and ending, a representation of self-possession and a visual elegy. The photograph is included in the book as a sign of the questions Trethewey travels with: How do we contend with the various and multiple archives of loss? What does it mean to stay true to them when, like this photograph, they can be interpreted so many ways? And how might she understand evidence like this one—her mother's picture— alongside her mother's other final photograph, the state's recorded image of her mother's murdered body?

Trethewey's book is written against the lure of forgetting, the desire to flee the scene of violence, to move and never look back. This is perhaps most poignantly visible in her description of her mother's record collection, one that Trethewey "jettisoned" after her mother's murder because it was "cargo I could not bear to carry."[39] The albums are gone now, Trethewey tells her readers, but "to have it now . . . might bring some part of her back, hundreds of albums that would play like the soundtrack to the story of her life, the years she lived, taking me back to the moment she first started collecting them."[40] That heavy cargo, that weight she could not carry, feels different now. She tells her readers, "I want all of it," particularly one—Funkadelic's *Maggot Brain*. Trethewey remembers an image from the cover of the LP—a woman with a large afro buried in dirt, her mouth open; she is screaming. And on the other side of the cover, an image: a skull. For Trethewey, this image—like the photograph of her mother—is haunting, "as if to show me the truth of my mother's life those years, foreshadowing what was to come."[41] The LPs, the "cargo," become something that Tretheway wanted to set aside in a desire to live a different life, to author herself anew. As she writes, "For a long time I tried to forget as much as I could of the twelve years between 1973 and 1985. I wanted to banish that part of my past, an act of self-creation by which I sought to be made only of what I consciously chose to remember . . . *But* there is a danger in willed forgetting; too much can be lost. It's been harder for me to call back my mother when I needed to most."[42] The memoir and its commitment to staying at the bone—sitting with the various records and memories of loss—is an effort to "call back" her mother and to recognize how none of these archives holds or captures her. Each is fragmentary; each is imperfect; each is marked by its own elisions.

It is Trethewey's return to Atlanta on the anniversary of her mother's murder that inaugurates her engagement with the official archives of loss. As Trethewey narrates it, a man recognizes her in a restaurant, and they begin to talk. He finally discloses that he was the first police officer to respond to her mother's murder and that since it has been twenty years since her mother's death, the state's archive is going to be destroyed. He tells Trethewey that if she wants to see this archive, it has to be soon. She writes, "I had willingly come back to this place, put myself in proximity to the events of my past. I'd even bought a house in walking distance of the courthouse . . . How could I think my past would not revisit me in countless ways? That I could go unrecognized in this place?"[43] Trethewey finds herself embedded in a place that requires her to contend with the past, to an archive of her mother's injuries and subsequent murder, to her own desire to forget and later to remember, and to what the official archive includes and erases.

There are records: transcripts, an autopsy, statements. And they promise Trethewey the opportunity to hear her mother speak, as in the case of one chapter that Trethewey calls "last words." This chapter consists of a twelve-page handwritten document Trethewey's mother wrote to officially recount the physical abuse she had suffered. The district attorney encouraged Trethewey's mother to record her husband's threats so that the state would have sufficient evidence to arrest him. The recording captured those threats and offered enough evidence to obtain an arrest warrant and a mandate that a police officer be stationed outside her mother's apartment. The officer who was supposed to be there, though, left in the early morning hours, precisely the time when Trethewey's mother was murdered. How close her mother came to safety, how close this official act of recordkeeping was to keeping her alive, and how spectacularly it failed. Staying close to the bone. The promise of that moment—the promise of being kept safe—and the truth of that moment: the state's failure. The transcript then was imagined to be evidence that would produce safety and is instead evidence of loss, of failure, of state neglect. It is evidence of everything that failed her mother. But, Trethewey's memoir requires us to ask: What does this transcript offer the daughter who longs for closeness with what has been lost?

Trethewey's memoir closes with an italicized paragraph so stunning that I reproduce it here in its entirety. It is a different kind of staying at the bone, one that refuses the official record in favor of another one: memory. Memory can be imperfect, gauzy, romantic; it is often revised and subject to the desires that shape the moment in which we access it. Like with Alexander's dreams, like with Ward's deep belief in the prospect of witnessing, there is this paragraph that stays at the bone differently. It stays at the bone of desire; it is beautifully faithful to a daughter's profound longings:

> *Often, when I am alone on the road, I think of traveling back to Mississippi each summer with my mother. The year before I was old enough to drive, she let me practice steering the car on long stretches of empty highway. I'd reach across the center console and take the wheel, leaning into her, my back against her chest, following the arc of the sun west toward home. For several miles we'd drive like that: so close we seemed conjoined, and I could feel her heart beating against me as if I had not one, but two.*[44]

So close we were conjoined.
Not one heart, but two.
The way that being "alone on the road"—even now—brings back the memory of the long drive, the "arc of the sun," the "empty highway," that

sensation of feeling someone else's heart beating against your own, and the magnitude and depths of that loss. This exists only in the archive of the remembered, but Trethewey reveals the power of that, at times, silent archive too, and how staying close to it can be a form of "calling back." She also shows us a different kind of evidence, an evidence of desire and memory, of "calling back" and longing. She reveals to her readers how this kind of time travel steeped in the tender and terrible longing for someone who is gone is also a kind of staying at the bone.

Staying With

In a memoir written in the wake of losing her father, Chimamanda Ngozi Adichie writes, "Grief is not gauzy; it is substantial, oppressive, a thing opaque. The weight is heaviest in the mornings, post-sleep: a leaden heart, a stubborn reality that refuses to budge. I will never see my father again. Never again. It feels as if I wake up only to sink and sink. In those moments, I am sure that I do not ever want to face the world again."[45] The texts that I write about here grapple with the "substance" and heft of loss by honoring an ethic of staying at the bone. They refuse metaphor and abstraction in favor of detail—whether the sound of a ventilator, the curve of a penis, or a close look at a mother's final portrait, one that was taken with no knowledge of what was to come. They insist on returning to the scene of loss—sometimes literally, as in Trethewey's return to Atlanta, and sometimes in dreamscapes, as in Alexander's description of how she still dreams of her husband, his hand in hers, and then the two of them moving apart. And they do this work of staying at the bone through a preoccupation with mothering, whether Ward's reflections on losing her Beloved, the father of her children; Trethewey's reflections on the "conjoined-ness" of her and her mother; or Alexander's ruminations on her husband's penis as that "with which we actually made the human beings who are our children." These texts insist that this kind of attention to loss is a form of living-with, a "lifeboat," that refuses forgetting and fleeing and that continues a conversation, a companionship, between the dead and the living. Yet they also suggest that the materiality of the bone can take myriad forms—staying at the bone can mean honoring dream, memory and its imperfection, fantasy, and the idea of fate.

I offer this rumination on proximity not to pathologize or condemn forgetting, or a strategic distance between ourselves and the objects we lose, but instead to point to how these authors remember—and remember on the page—as a form of living and as a practice of living with those they have lost. It is a complicated lifeboat, one that can be both a source of companionship and something that undoes its author, as when Trethewey describes being surrounded by the material evidence of her mother's murder and letting out a deep and visceral wail. But this is the risk of writing at the bone—it can bring us to our knees, to the moment when the only thing we can do is let out a guttural moan as we remember all that has been lost and all the living that has happened without those who have been lost.

In this chapter I study a contemporary Black feminist push toward witnessing and proximity, toward closeness—even if unbearable closeness—as a way of doing justice to loss. I track the call to live with loss, to live *next to* loss, rather than the call to outlive it, as a contemporary Black feminist preoccupation. And I am also interested in the promises that getting close can be a lifeboat, a form of shelter, a practice of safety, even as it can also unravel us (and our readers), leaving us exposed, vulnerable, and shaken, and even as the proximity can never return the lost object, can never undo the trauma, and perhaps can only take us to the scene of loss again and again.

The refusal of distance is its own form of relentless labor, even as it is a way of communing with the dead, offering them companionship. Alexander thinks with this question explicitly as she asks, "How much space for remembering is there in a day? How much should there be? I think about this in my poetry. I don't want to be a nostalgist. Yet I feed on memory, need it to make poems, the art that is made of the stuff I have; my life and the world around me."[46]

I feed on memory.

What does it mean to be fed by memory, to consume it, and even to need it for sustenance? And how might we contend with the fictions of memory—questions Trethewey thinks through so beautifully in her always-recognition of the imperfections and "revisions" of remembering, again that line from Elizabeth Spires—memory is false as anything but, she tells us, better than forgetting. (Is it? Always?)[47] Perhaps, Alexander suggests, staying at the bone is honoring memory as not a retrospective gaze but a method of being in the present, a mode of living. It is a willingness to document even those most intimate places that loss touches, to graze the wound with our fingers—an act that can be both tender and painful. It is a refusal to leave loss alone, even for a second.

*

Stay at the bone.
What is that book you're reading? My mother asks.
The Light of the World.
Is it good?
Yes, it's good.
I'd love to read it sometime. Can I borrow it sometime?
Yes, of course. Any time.
Is it good?
Yes, it's good.
I'd love to read it sometime.

3

An Invitation to Listen

My mother called me a *nosy child*. I would place an empty glass against a closed door to hear adult conversations. I would hold mail up to the light to catch a glimpse of what was inside the envelope. I kept binoculars on my bedside table and stared into our neighbor's bedroom. I would piece together evidence and observe patterns. I would notice when a piece of information—however innocuous—was withheld.

It was no help that my father was compulsively private. He would take conversations in the basement—"Hold on," he would say to whomever was on the other end of the call—and then he would walk slowly downstairs to the mildewy basement with its peeling green walls. He called this dimly lit space his office. He had a desk that could barely fit a legal pad, an answering machine, two perfectly sharpened pencils, and an exercise mat that he would unroll on Sundays to do push-ups. And it is from that desk that he would "take a call," in what seemed to me to be a conspiratorial whisper. I would stand on the other side of the shut door. I would close my eyes so that I could focus on listening. I felt if I closed my eyes as tightly as I could stand, the sound would improve.

It was also no help that for much of my adolescence, my parents were in the long middle of their marriage, a time when it seemed that our family might not hold. As an only child, my survival, I thought, hinged on eavesdropping. I would listen to my parents' whispered fights to try to gather some sense of what the future, *our* future, might hold. Even in the moment when my parents and I hugged each other in front of my freshman dorm on Massachusetts Avenue, we collectively set off into a future that was entirely unknowable. I could not fathom what might happen to them, to us. I didn't know if they would find something to sustain them beyond their shared Black middle-class aspirations for future generations—for me, really. My father and I are the only people on this earth who remember that time, and it is the one thing we do not discuss. As the years have passed, we have become more alike: our preoccupations, our identically shaped bodies and patterns of speech. But this remains the silence between us: the story of what almost happened between my parents, and how it didn't happen.

Nosy child, nosy adult. I always wondered about the shoebox in my parents' basement, the one where my father—the family archivist—had kept (in chronological order) every letter my mother mailed him from Vassar College. Truth be told, he was with her for much of the time she was a student at Vassar. He would hitchhike to Poughkeepsie from New York City every week. He was there often enough that many of my mother's classmates thought he was one of the few men enrolled in what Vassar describes as its first fully coeducational class.[1] My father was two years older than my mother, but he had spent his first and second years of college moving from school to school (he is the only person who holds the history of why this happened, and it is one that he seems reluctant to share). By the time he met my mother—the summer before her first year at Vassar—he was prepared to begin his freshman year again at City College of New York. There was no courting, really. From what they tell me, he declared himself her boyfriend, and she accepted. He spent the next four years hitchhiking back and forth from New York City to Poughkeepsie, until he saved enough money to buy a small yellow car that made a ticking noise. My mother reports she could hear my father a few blocks away, and it allowed her enough time to slip her jacket on and get outside before his car rolled up. From what I can tell, the few days each week when she was left to the company of her friends and the ordinary rhythms of school, she would write to my father. These letters lived in my parents' basement for forty years.

That box of letters had always been tantalizing. I knew of its existence, but I had also heard my father's warning: *That box is private.* I have long wanted to see their romance, to have access to a story of the immensity of their affection in the years before their shared project became launching me. My mother's Vassar yearbook is a testament to the sexual revolution unfolding in real time. I grew up flipping through it and my impression of college was formed by it—many of her classmates posed naked in their senior photos. My mother's picture appears toward the back of the book on a page called "just regular folks." She wears a black turtleneck with a silver sequined spiderweb across her chest. Her hair is long and ironed straight, parted in the middle, a gesture to the times—this was 1974. Everything else, though, is against the moment: the turtleneck and the embarrassed smile. I hoped that in the shoebox, in those letters, she might seem as unbuttoned as her classmates appeared in those pictures: desirous, playful, sexual. But I never approached that box in my parents' house, despite my will to read, my desire to know.

The shoebox of letters didn't make it to Chapel Hill, North Carolina, when my parents left—*escaped* might be the right word—their life in New Jersey, and the house that was organized around their working lives in New York City, professional identities that were shed with their respective retirements. Somehow, they packed up forty years of brochures, plastic bags, good-enough wire hangers, outdated clothing, and about thirty dozen small bottles of hotel shampoo and conditioner and moved it to North Carolina, where I spent the good part of a summer sorting it. My father was in a frenzy at the end of their month of packing. The final boxes he packed are a testament to his fatigue; one contained four wire hangers, some trash bags, a collection of seashells, and a Nutribullet. What I don't know is what happened to the shoebox, if it was tossed into a dumpster or if it remains hidden somewhere in the small storage unit in the basement of their new apartment building. What I have found is just one letter, this one penned not by my mother but by my father.

Imagine what I discovered: He was then as he is now. His letter is marked by a deep and sustained attention to the mundane. My father has long been attuned to the portions of a story that the rest of us edit out: standing in line in a store, the price of gasoline, the pothole on the corner, the circular that came in the mail, a credit card that was applied for, a coupon promising a minuscule discount. Life lived on the small scale.

I often tell a story of my first trip to India, waking up in my in-laws' house—disoriented and jet-lagged—to the sound of cawing crows and the distant pounding of hammering. I called my father and said, "Dad, we're here." And he said, "Good, good. Now I want to tell you something important. Remember that pothole on the corner of Cranford and Grayson?" He waits as if about to deliver the punch line of a joke: "It's still there, Jen. It's still there."

So here I am: I wanted access to something about my mother, an archive of her barely post-adolescent desire, and I instead encounter my father. I am left only to imagine my mother, the letter's recipient, opening the envelope and reading his careful cursive. How did a twenty-year-old woman interpret her boyfriend's steadfast commitment to the mundane? Was it a sign of his reliability, his commitment to the everyday, or perhaps a sign of his dullness? It is a fantasy to think I could have ever asked these questions and gotten answers, of course.

But there is no posing these questions now.

Last night we ate Chinese takeout. My mother opens the Styrofoam containers and scoops eggplant and basil onto her plate. She eats happily and then looks lovingly at me and compliments me on the meal she thinks I have prepared. I am elated that she has enjoyed the food. I am devastated that she has already forgotten that I haven't cooked this food. Life is filled with the evidence of slowly losing her.

This is when my eavesdropping impulse is at its strongest. And yet I know it cannot be satisfied. Now I cannot press my ear to any doors. There is nothing to listen to that will offer me a glimpse into the past. Instead, there is one letter and all my desires to hold on to the present and to touch the past, to have what feels like one last chance to get to know my mother.

Forms of Address

In 2019 Imani Perry published *Breathe*. The book is a letter addressed to her sons, Freeman and Issa, and is animated by a mother's abiding wish for her sons to keep breathing. This is a wish voiced in a moment when "I can't breathe" had become a rallying call for the movement for Black life and a collective "wake work." Perry's *Breathe* is a letter written in anticipation of loss, one that treats preparation for grief as the hallmark of contemporary Black maternal life. Perry writes, "Something distinct has happened in your time. It is the product of camera phones, the diminishing whiteness of America, the backlash against a Black presidency, the persistence of American racism, the money-making weapons industry, the value added of murder in police dossiers, law-and-order policing."[2] This is a familiar story: about Black sons, about the times we live in and how they are both a deep continuation of the past and distinct in the new visibility of Black death. This story takes on what has now become a familiar Black feminist form: the letter.

Five years earlier, in August 2014, Sybrina Fulton—Trayvon Martin's mother—published a letter to Michael Brown's family in *TIME* magazine.[3] The letter was written two years after Martin was fatally shot and a year after

George Zimmerman was acquitted of second-degree murder and manslaughter in Martin's death. It was published two weeks after Michael Brown's murder, in the days when Ferguson, Missouri, became synonymous with a newly visible Black Lives Matter movement and with what many news sources decried as "civil unrest."[4] Fulton described the immensity of her grief at the fact that the Brown family would "join this exclusive yet growing group of parents and relatives who have lost loved ones to senseless gun violence."[5] She advised them to "surround yourselves with proven and trusted support. . . . I have always said that Trayvon was not perfect. But no one will ever convince me that my son deserved to be stalked and murdered. No one can convince you that Michael deserved to be executed."[6] And she suggested—as she did many times in the months following her son's murder—that her son's death was the birth of her political consciousness.[7] She instructed the Brown family, "If they refuse to hear us, we will make them feel us. . . . [F]eeling us means feeling our pain; imagining our plight as parents of slain children."[8]

These two letters—one taking the form of a book and one published in a magazine—are my point of departure in this chapter. I study how Black feminists use the form of the letter to make Black loss—particularly Black maternal loss—"felt" by its readers. This body of work insists that the form of the letter makes Black maternal loss particularly feelable by transporting its reader to the scene of loss.[9] In the book's first chapter, I talked about how the beautiful voice this book centers is made through repetition, and this chapter thinks about how ubiquitous the letter form has become, how it is now the primary vehicle for describing Black loss to a broad public. If Jack Hamilton describes the "open letter" as "the most overused mode of contemporary writing, a one-sided conversation with someone famous in which the performative bypass of audience creates an aloof sort of anti-intimacy," Emily Lordi insists that "for black writers in particular, working in an embattled political moment, the epistolary form offers a way to address the effects of racial oppression without centering those who perpetuate and benefit from it."[10] I draw on Lordi's insights on the importance of the letter in an "embattled political moment," tracing how Black feminists strategically deploy the letter to produce intimacy and proximity with readers, to transport readers to the scene of loss, to make Black maternal grief "feelable."[11]

In making this claim, I ask how contemporary Black feminist authors work to transform their readers into eavesdroppers. They invite readers to get as close as possible to a whispering voice. Letters allow their readers to have the sensation—perhaps exciting, perhaps risky, perhaps uncomfortable—of reading something that didn't anticipate them. Of course, these letters *did* anticipate a broad reading public, as in the case of Perry's book or Fulton's *TIME* magazine publication. But the form of the letter allows readers to feel—however fleetingly—that they are encountering something that did not foresee their readership. The feeling of being an eavesdropper is a device, and a profound one, that Black feminists have mobilized with a particular intensity in the period of Black Lives Matter. And it is a device that has been deployed precisely because it is imagined to render Black loss knowable in a distinct way.

In using the term *eavesdropping*, I recognize that I deploy it differently than others. I am describing the act of *reading* something that did not anticipate us rather than hearing something that did not anticipate us as a practice of eavesdropping. Or perhaps I am suggesting that the act of reading and the act of listening are simply not that distinct. If in the first chapter, I talked about how beautiful writing is marked by various forms of seduction, the letter makes this particularly visible. Readers are allowed to feel—encouraged to feel, even—like they are accessing an intimate conversation that did not intend their listening. But, of course, the letter is consciously constructed and staged, performed for its reader, all the while hiding its performative qualities.

My understanding of eavesdropping is informed by Krista Ratcliffe's celebration of eavesdropping as a "tactic for listening to the discourse of others, for hearing over the edges of our own knowing, for thinking what is commonly unthinkable within our own logics."[12] For Ratcliffe, eavesdropping is a feminist tactic aligned with listening, "world-traveling," and attending to a politics of location.[13] I think about eavesdropping differently, treating it not entirely in the romantic register of resistance. While I think eavesdropping can invite forms of generative listening, I am also curious about why Black maternal pain must be made feelable in certain ways to be visible, to be engaged. I also explore the kinds of Black loss that become consumable (and marketable), the kinds that the letter repeats. I am equally interested in why Black feminists want readers to *feel* like they are "hearing over the edges of [their] own knowing." I aspire to understand why Black feminists have steadfastly imagined that making Black women's losses knowable—something that is imagined as a necessary precondition to a cultural recognition of Black women's full and "complex personhood"—requires Black women to lay bare their secrets, or at least to pretend to do so.[14] Thus I sit with Lordi's important insight that the epistolary is always marked by the "demand that writers balance two aims: of 'enlightening' the dominant culture and of sharing tactics of survival with loved ones and others under siege."[15] I think about how contemporary Black feminist writers negotiate these competing demands and how they grapple with a complex wish to render Black maternal loss knowable to a broad public.

The archive of contemporary Black feminist letters that I think with here builds on and reinterprets the intellectual and political insights of Ta-Nehisi Coates's celebrated *Between the World and Me* (2015). Following James Baldwin's *The Fire Next Time*, Coates's book is a letter written to his fifteen-year-old son. *Between the World and Me* was penned in direct response to the enduring conditions of racism and the newly visible conditions of anti-Black violence (the publisher moved its release date earlier, so that the book could circulate in the wake of the white supremacist mass shooting committed by Dylann Roof in a Charleston, South Carolina, church in 2015). Coates begins his letter with a diagnosis of the present moment, which has inaugurated a new global consciousness of Black death and a new market for literary works that document Black mourning. He writes, "This was the year you saw Eric Garner choked to death for selling cigarettes; because you know now that Renisha McBride was shot for seeking help, that John Crawford was shot down for browsing in a department store. And you have seen men in uniform drive by and murder Tamir Rice, a twelve-year-old child whom they were oath-bound to protect."[16] Garner, McBride, Crawford, and Rice are, for Coates, key entries in a contemporary glossary of Black death. Their names are ways of narrating a present moment marked by the simultaneous not-newness of Black death and the newness of cultural attention to Black death. They are also a way of narrating his son's emerging consciousness of the precarity of Black life, and of instructing his son on American "heritage": a predilection for "destroy[ing] the black body."[17] Ultimately, Coates presents his son—his readers, really—with what he calls the "question of my life": "how one should live within a black body, within a country lost in the Dream."[18] How, he asks, can his son, and his readers, live in history, *with* a recognition of American "inheritance," and carve out a space for Black living, self-invention, and tenderness?

Coates's book—his wish for his son's freedom expressed as a letter—became the defining text of the early days of Black Lives Matter, what Brit Bennett described as "a crucial book during this moment of generational awakening."[19] And it is one that used the form of the letter—the pretense of an intergenerational conversation between a father and son—to allow its reader to eavesdrop, to hear a conversation about dispossession, violence, anticipation, and grief. Michelle Alexander highlights Coates's use of address and construction of audience in her review of the book. She notes that *Between the World and Me* is "not addressed to white people. The usual hedging and filtering and softening and overall distortion that seems to happen automatically—even unconsciously—when black people attempt to speak about race to white people in public is absent."[20] Of course, the book *did* anticipate white readers, and Hamilton insists that the book is "written toward white Americans, and I say this as one of them. White Americans may need to read this book more urgently and carefully than anyone, and their own sons and daughters need to read it as well."[21] What made *Between the World and Me* distinctly able to speak Black loss differently was that it took the form of an intimate conversation. It allowed its readers to *feel* as if they were eavesdropping on a conversation that they may—or may not—have access to otherwise. This proximity allowed readers to encounter familiar terrain anew, with a new sense of an intimate understanding of anti-Black violence. *Between the World and Me* has since become central to the anti-racist reading project of 2020 (which, by 2022, when I write this chapter, had already begun to disappear).[22]

In the years since Coates's celebrated book was published, in the midst of what has been described as a Black Lives Matter literary market, Black feminists have laid claim to the epistolary and made it a primary form for naming and describing a particular kind of Black maternal loss, for ensuring that this loss is seen and felt. To be clear, I begin with Coates not to suggest that he inaugurated a form that Black feminists have copied; instead, I track how Black feminists have deployed and remade the form of the letter, harnessing its intimate power and centering the Black maternal as the key icon of Black loss. This is not simply a "say her name" response to Coates's masculinist approach—an ethics that was highlighted and critiqued even as the book was celebrated.[23] It is a deployment of the form of the letter, and its performance of intimacy, to fundamentally restage the paradigmatic Black loss *not* as the Black father losing his Black son but as the Black mother losing her Black son.

This chapter begins by thinking more deeply about the letter and its prominent place in a Black feminist Black Lives Matter archive. I am particularly invested in the letter's promise to bring us to the scene of loss, and in the kinds of loss that are revealed to readers, and in the ways that all of this unfolds through the pretext of intimacy. The remainder of the chapter thinks about other ways the Black feminist letter might work, to think loss differently with a particular attention to the ordinary, the quiet, the quotidian. I study Julietta Singh's *The Breaks*, an extended letter to her daughter. Singh draws on Black feminist theory—particularly Saidiya Hartman's

Lose Your Mother—to think rigorously and beautifully about forms of nonspectacular, durational, and ordinary loss and to reimagine loss as anticipated and expected but also welcome and generative. When I describe my desire to think apart from the now dominant performance of Black loss, it is not an impulse to critique or condemn Black feminist work on grief and loss, particularly on the anticipated loss of Black sons. Instead, I want to think with Black feminist theory to open up space for other kinds of Black loss and grief, those that are ordinary, complicated, surprising, and those that move in slow motion. I want to make room for forms of Black loss that have different relationships to privacy and publicity, those that refuse spectacle and are inhabited in the everyday, which might make them take on different registers and shapes. I turn to Singh's work, then, not out of a desire to supplant or replace Black feminist texts that offer us important ways of thinking about the conditions of the present, but instead because it points us toward the complex and multifaceted itineraries of loss. I look to Singh's book to think with performances of loss and intimacies of loss that center unknowability, uncertainty, mystery, and even forms of pleasure and solidarity.

Black Feminist Letters

The letter has become ubiquitous, a device for naming forms of Black grief and anticipated loss. Like "the talk"—often described as the painful conversation Black parents are required to have with their children, particularly their sons, about navigating routine anti-Black state violence—the letter has become a well-traveled form allowing a constructed public display of Black pain and grief, a way of describing the temporality of anticipation. While I mention "the talk"—another entry in a larger cultural lexicon of Black grief—the talk operates differently than the letter. On an NPR episode devoted to the talk, Kenya Young notes:

> I'll never forget there was a time—the kids wanted to go to the park. This was right around the time of Philando Castile and Alton Sterling. My third son was just born. And I had many moments where I was holding him or nursing him and crying as I did so. Because, while I loved this little bundle of joy immensely, also just the amount of fear and worry for who I just brought into the world again, another Black son, and the burdens that I have to carry with that again. It was really raw for me around that time.[24]

For Young, the talk is a shorthand for a required form of Black maternal vigilance. The talk is a way of describing the dreaded parental labor of preparing children for forms of violence that are expected and routinized, and a shorthand for detailing how Black children are robbed of the idea of childhood innocence that continues to structure whiteness.[25]

But the letter shifts us from a description of a conversation between parents and children to an opportunity for readers to *hear* that conversation—or at least to feel that they are hearing it. Eavesdropping. This is a performance of an intimate conversation between mothers and children made visible for readers' consumption. And the letter has proliferated, appearing in magazines, newspapers, and books, and read aloud on radio stations, making eavesdropping a prevailing experience of engaging Black loss.[26] In "A Radical Love Letter to My Son," for example, Sarah Mantilla Griffin speaks directly to her son: "In the wake of the killing of Trayvon Martin and the acquittal of his killer, my phone, email, and Facebook feed lit up with the concerns of mothers like myself, asking: how do we keep our children safe?... Loving you—who will constantly be at risk of physical and psychological injury—is perilous, but I wholeheartedly believe that it is a powerful way to enable you to be whole."[27] Griffin details the "risk" of Black mothering of Black boys: the threat of loss paired with the decision to move forward with "radical" love, a form of love that requires "nothing less than our selves in the pursuit of a revolution that begins with our children's mental and physical health and ends with those children transforming our country and our world."[28] But she insists, as she writes in the first sentences of the letter, "I love you. I have chosen how to love you. I love you radically, and I hope that this love will keep you free."[29]

Joy Sewing's editorial in the *Houston Chronicle*, also in the form of a letter to her son, begins with the acknowledgment that he cannot understand the letter she is writing. She notes, "At just 4, you are too young to understand what his death has meant to the world, too young to know that his [Martin's] life amplified dissidence."[30] In fact, her son becomes a literary device, one that allows her to imagine a future conversation that her readers can access, a conversation about living and loss, about anticipation and grief. What does it mean, her letter requires its readers to ask, to anticipate talking to a small child about state violence and future loss? Despite the fact that she notes her son cannot "understand what [Martin's] death has meant to the world," Sewing uses the letter to document the feelings of loss and anticipation that already mark her daily life, which she argues are constitutive of Black maternal life. The letter becomes a vehicle for capturing how loss already constitutes the present tense of Black maternal life. She writes, "I want to immerse myself into your soccer games and Cub Scouts meetings, your school dances and first dates. But they are all weighted in the reality that your life often is not considered to be of value. My job is to spread my arms wide to shield you from that."[31] To make oneself into a shield, Sewing notes, is the work of the Black maternal. And the everyday of Black maternal life is that soccer games and Cub Scouts meetings and the joyful banal become steeped in vigilance and anxiety. Reflecting on the anniversary of Martin's death, she reminds her son—her readers—"I wish I could say things are getting better, but that would not be true."[32] The form of the letter becomes a crucial way of naming the unchanging same with a different kind of intimacy, with the added emotional pull of imagining a mother describing loss, trauma, and grief to a child not yet old enough, perhaps, to fully understand the weight of that grief.

Perry's *Breathe* is part of this tradition: Perry speaks to her sons, describing what it means to mother them with the threat of imminent loss and to live with the singular wish for her sons to live on. It is an account of loss that is both rooted in the everyday and attuned to the spectacular, to how state violence erupts in and ruptures the ordinary. She writes, "The everyday. The homework, the cooking, the cleaning, the activities, the practices, the friends, the rearing, it is so much—even, or perhaps because of, the choices and things I have been afforded. And then, on top of that, the daily work of beating back the ugliness. And reconciliation with the irreconcilable. You live in some worlds that are more white than Black. And so, you learn, early on, that the aversion to Blackness can turn perfectly lovely people grotesque."[33] The anticipation that attends to Black mothering is embedded in "the cooking, the cleaning, the activities," it is routine, and yet as it is lived and feared, it is also spectacular. And while she refuses the logic of "this could have been my child," insisting that "my children are here, and they stand with me, to honor their dead," the book is about a wish that Elizabeth Alexander describes as "magical thinking," the wish for Black boys' living in the face of a world that thrives on devouring black people.[34]

And magical thinking, this genre reveals, is often about wishing, wanting, desiring in a world where Black dreaming is so often rendered impossible. Perry makes clear her own longings for her sons. She writes, "I want to hold you safe. I also want you to fly. . . . Yes, I am asking you to do something difficult. To make beauty and love in a genocidal time, with a harrowing past behind you."[35] The idea of flying Black boys channels Toni Morrison's *Song of Solomon* and Alexander's own image of dancing Black boys as an imagining of some kind of Black freedom, or at least an embodied representation of what Joshua Chambers-Letson calls "More Life."[36] Perry's wish is for mobility, for freedom in one's body, for the feeling of possibility and imagination. And she names other wishes for mobility, which seem to be central to mitigating loss; as she says, "I would like to take you to Africa one day. I am one of those Black people who believes in the value of return. However, you have already been to your ancestral home many times. It is the Deep South . . . The we to which you belong was born in the South of the United States."[37] Movement becomes a way of imagining something other than loss, grief, and death, a way of thinking about what Black life might look like if it were not already constituted by the ordinariness and regularity of violence.

And yet, at the very end of the book, Perry surprisingly breaks the form of the letter, addressing the reader directly about the decision to craft her book as a letter. This rupture feels surprising, jarring even, in a book that has allowed its readers to eavesdrop, to listen to Perry speak to her sons. It is this break that I want to sit with. She narrates a conversation where her editor asked her if she would be interested in writing a book that took the form of a letter to her sons. She writes, "I know the power of letters. I have received and written them my whole life."[38] The idea of letters as having a "power" comes, at least in part, from the intimate voice they construct, from how they whisper in their readers' ears. But even as she recognizes that letters wield a certain amount of power, that they mobilize intimacy for rhetorical force, she maintains that her letter is not merely a literary device, that "my sons are real in my life, and this is really for them."[39] In other words, while her sons appear on the page as characters, as literary and political devices that allow her to elaborate on anti-Blackness, they are, she contends, "real," and the book is "really for them," not for us, the readers, the eavesdroppers. Even as she insists on the particularity of her sons, and the book as an offering to her children, she also claims the general applicability of her book, noting, "If I had had your child instead of mine, the heart of what I said would repeat, though its elaboration moved by circumstance."[40] While Perry breaks from the letter here, she elaborates one of the most significant rhetorical moves the letter advances: it can at once insist on the radical specificity of its recipient and claim to speak broadly and generally. It is both about Perry's sons and about the precarity of all Black boys. It allows her to claim that "every second-person sentence devoted to them in these pages is to all of us. It is received wisdom from their witness and passionate hope for their futures."[41] The book can both address her sons and speak to "all of us" and our shared futures.

There are, of course, substantial costs to the public performance of Black women's grief, costs that Perry has taken up in other forms outside of the letter. Indeed, I suggest that in her insistence that her book is about her "real in my life" sons, that the book is "really" written for them, Perry gestures to the complexities of Black performances of intimacy for public consumption, and even for a public anti-racist pedagogy. Perry's conversation with Samaria Rice, Tamir Rice's mother, finds Perry advocating that scholars and activists think critically about "hustling Black death." Perry writes, "In a sense, [Samaria] Rice wanted to maintain her authority over both her own voice and her son's legacy. To an extent, this was never possible. Although Tamir was her child, when we saw his sweet face emblazoned across our televisions, he became everyone's . . . She became particularly animated as she described those who make a living 'hustling Black death.' From where she sits, she sees 'book deals, movie deals.' Cocking her head to the side, as if speaking directly to her adversaries, she adds, 'What was you doing?'"[42] In posing the question "What was you doing?" Samaria Rice asks what happens when a child—*her* child—becomes "everyone's child," when one's grief becomes felt (or claimed to be felt) by so many. The notion of Tamir Rice as "everyone's child"—the notion of Black children as "community property"—has been a key strategy advocated not just by Perry but by others in their desire to claim some semblance of innocence for Black children, and in their collective impulse to ensure "More Life" for Black boys.[43] Indeed, in *Breathe*, Perry positions her sons as always fiercely her own, and also as characters who appear on the page to make a larger argument about the need to preserve Black male breath. Her sons appear in the form of the letter—which allows readers to intimately access anticipated pain—precisely because Perry wants us to imagine the terror of losing them, and the particular terror of approaching this fear repeatedly. But for Rice, this positioning of Black boys as collectively held is not exclusively a form of radical politics. It is also another theft, which she describes as "benefitting off the blood" of her child.[44] Rice emphasizes that the public performance of Black privacy—precisely the logic that undergirds the now ubiquitous Black feminist letter—actually produces its own set of losses. Her intervention requires us to ask, What happens when even your grief gets taken, or feels as if it is? Or when it circulates in ways that make it unrecognizable? This might be one version of what Dagmawi Woubshet describes as "compounding loss," but here the accumulation of loss happens in the name of Black freedom.[45]

I offer Rice's critical and challenging queries about loss and ownership—and the economies that have sprung up around Black loss—without resolution. Instead, I see her words as requiring us to contend with the costs of performances of intimacy and proximity that render "real" dead and dying people community property whose names and stories can be circulated for a host of political reasons. As Rice suggests, when her son's name or image is used—regardless of political rationale—it is a theft; it is yet another experience of loss, a sense that even her grief is not her own. We might, then, think of whether the letter is its own "hustling" of Black death, one staged for making visible persistent violence, one enacted to give a name and a feeling to what Black women have long lived with. But it is, of course, a performance that allows its readers to get close, to eavesdrop, to feel a proximity to pain that may or may not be their own. And as Rice suggests, this performance requires, at the very least, that we grapple with its ethics, that we think about its consequences. It is a performance that asks that we contend with whether Black women's grief and loss might be feelable in other ways, made felt, made visible, and even with how we might contest the notion that we must show our wounds over and over again to prove their reality. It also requires that we think about the political desire to make Black loss feelable—for whom, and under what conditions.

Breaking

The Black feminist letter can also be used to offer conceptions of loss that emphasize the ordinary and the nonspectacular, the quiet and the processual, and that think about loss and its complex circuits differently. In this section I study Julietta Singh's *The Breaks* (2021). Singh draws on Hartman's analysis of Black historical loss to think about maternal loss as a productive *and* disruptive mode of living, as a form of self-making, and as a generative process of imagining a different and more livable world. To be clear, Singh is making a break from Hartman even as she builds on her work. If Hartman thinks about the collective Black loss of motherland and home—a loss that can never be repaired—Singh thinks about mother loss as "the political act of culling from history and discarding what does not serve you" and as a project of self-invention and self-forging.[46] Singh's work is indebted to Black feminist theory even as she emphasizes that she engages with a robust archive of Black feminist theoretical work as a brown mother, and as a brown mother of a brown daughter.

Singh's *The Breaks* is an extended letter. But Singh writes to her daughter—not, as is the tradition of the Black feminist letter that I narrate, to a son. She begins by telling her daughter, "I am writing to you, and to future you. I am writing to the six-year-old girl you are now, the one who both insists on her unequivocal need for my body and loves to perform her independence from me."[47] The letter, Singh reveals, is always about writing to a present "you" and an imagined future "you," about the time she is in and a future time she imagines. And the future Singh imagines is a dark one—again, much as the other letters I write about here mark an anticipation of future destruction. But for Singh, this is a future marked by ecological catastrophe, by the collapse of democratic institutions, by our collective death. Singh is interested in the feeling of the inevitable destruction that awaits us, a destruction that is much of our own making. As she notes:

> I write not with the immediate fear that you will be gunned down by police in the streets, or that you will be metabolized by the prison industrial complex, but with an adjacent set of fears about being a Brown girl in a country that thinks and feels race through a sharp binary. I write with an impossible desire to prepare you for political and ecological catastrophe. . . . I write because, as mother and daughter, we are unmistakably entwined, and because I know—which is to say I feel in the most microbial registers of my body—that the shape of our environment will need to be radically reformed as we fight global patriarchy, extractive capitalism, and indiscriminate planetary destruction.[48]

While Singh carefully describes the fears she does not have—including an "immediate fear" that her daughter "will be gunned down by police in the streets"—she also captures the fears that she thinks mark the collective and her daughter: the slow and fast times of "political and ecological catastrophe."[49]

The notion of living in the ongoing time of disaster—a time that unfolds in slow motion and at quick speed—permeates her book, alongside a sense that generational struggle to remake the world and even generational rupture is required if life is to continue. In other words, the only response to the ongoing catastrophes of the present is to break, to imagine otherwise. This is a generational story for Singh: children must break from their parents, young people must break from older generations, the world must be remade and remade again, and this struggle is welcome and necessary. Breaks are neither unexpected nor unwelcome; they are not necessarily forms of violence, though they can be experienced as injury and as ruptures that we grieve and mourn. But for Singh breaks are forms of living on that are particularly visible to mothers, who, she argues, are broken *from* by their children. The story she tells, in fact, about maternal life is that it is one of nurturing the breaks, of being ready for a maternal pain that she argues can be felt in a register adjacent to loss.

As Singh writes—channeling Hartman—"I know that we must lose our mothers, often only later (and in a perverse twist) to become them in ways we may not be able to predict or appreciate."[50] The sense that we *must* lose our mothers, that this loss is foundational and necessary, is a deep rearticulation of the dreaded anticipation of loss. For Singh, loss is expected, even if challenging and demanding. Singh's call to "lose our mothers" is not about violent capture and displacement, exile and racial violence; it is about differentiation and exploration, about self-imagining and self-fashioning. It is about self-making and world-making, and it is an insistence that some forms of loss are necessary for living on.

While Singh argues that we must "lose our mothers," make our own worlds apart from them, Singh's wish is that this break is staged with tenderness and care. She longs for breaks that produce something other than brokenness and perhaps even yield new forms of connection and love. This is the challenge of brown maternal life (and brown daughter life): to break gently, with tenderness and regard. As Singh writes, "Losing me, my way of life, is unquestionably a requisite to survival and futurity. Yet I hope with every thread of my being that this world-altering shift can become a form of breaking that does not sever us entirely, or wrench us into mutual unbelonging. My most intimate desire is that you find a way to break *with* me rather than to break *from* me. A desire in which the necessity of our breaking does not so much leave me behind in your struggle to survive as it invites me in and calls me to blaze alongside you."[51] While the break can be a form of loss, it can also be the beginning of new forms of relating and being together, what Singh calls an invitation to "blaze alongside you." What forms of relationality become possible when the hierarchical mother-daughter dyad is troubled, inverted, flipped, or wholly toppled? What does an invitation to "blaze alongside" each other look like when it is articulated from the vantage point of the daughter and felt from the position of the maternal? What might it mean to break in ways that do not produce "mutual unbelonging" but instead continue to make possible forms of urgent connection?

I find this sense that mother and daughter—brown mother and daughter—can "blaze together" an account of the maternal very much in line with Alice Walker's early articulation of her relationship with her daughter, whom she imagines not as property or as someone she dominates, but instead as "sister." This is a model of reproduction as a practice of co-existence rather than as seeking our replacement or enacting a will to dominate.

This notion of breaking *with* rather than *from*—breaking as a form of generative rupture rather than catastrophic failure—is the utopian impulse of Singh's book. For Singh, brown mothering is distinct not in its proximity to loss but in its capacity to nurture the breaks and to see them as productive rather than threatening. Singh writes, "You now have been reared through an explicitly Brown maternity. For now, and for the most part, your orientations stem from mine. I imagine these orientations as rhizomes sending out little shoots that will lead you far away from me. I can't even begin to anticipate where they might take you. I want to offer myself to you as a base, not so that you can build yourself up from a fantasy of solid ground, but so you can discover the breaks, cracks, and sinkholes that constitute the lives that came before you."[52] An "explicitly Brown maternity" is one that recognizes mothering as "sending out little shoots that will lead you far away from me." It is a sense that mothering is about both proximity and distance as measurements of love. It is also a commitment to treating maternal flesh as a "base" for allowing other forms of living and breathing to take hold.

I think with Singh because of how she uses the letter to narrate a form of brown loss that does not (yet) appear in the letters that begin this chapter, and because of how this narration unfolds alongside Black feminist theory, including Hartman's signature work on race, kinship, and rupture. I think through how loss becomes something that Singh sees as necessary and life-affirming, even as it might also be threatening and overwhelming. This multivalent form of loss fascinates me precisely because it captures the multiple forms and affects that loss can generate, the way it can feel sustaining and devastating simultaneously. I am also invested in how Singh uses the familiar form of the letter—key to how Black feminists have made public seemingly private loss—to offer another iteration of racialized loss, to think about loss that is slow rather than spectacular, that is not about theft but about growth.

To lose your mother, Singh argues, is part of the process of brown mothering and daughtering, part of living with each other. The threat of the break is that it offers distance and no possibility of intimacy. The promise is that a new world is possible. We might think of this as capturing all that is both risky and thrilling about being together. As she tells her daughter, "I desire never to lose you, but for the sake of life itself, I need you to lose me. At the end of this world, you will rightfully be angry about what I am not yet prepared to reject in this age of purported freedom. But I hope your anger will not lead you to abandon everything that came before you, that it does not prevent you from culling what is of use from history for the future you will strive toward."[53] Singh's call for a generative form of slow breaking that is about reimagining the world is a different conception of loss; she recognizes that the breaks still might register as pain for Black and brown mothers, who, in Singh's imaginary, must live with the threat of "abandonment" and the fierce hope that "your anger will not lead you to abandon everything that came before you." But even with the specter of abandonment and loss, there is the idea of breaking *with*, an idea of loss that the dominant Black feminist voice rarely offers because of its rehearsal of a singular vision of loss that is spectacular and tethered to a singular event, where loss is violent theft. Ultimately, I turn to Singh's letter—and its investment in borrowing Hartman's conception of "lose your mother"—to consider how Black feminist theory can retain its investment in proximity and intimacy while troubling a paradigm of loss that makes Singh's vision of the breaks hard to see from within the parameters of Black feminist thought. How, Singh asks us, might loss be a precondition for rethinking the world? How might loss position brown and Black mothers not as forever-bereaved, as icons of grief, but as people whose experiences of loss engender new forms of relationality that may be uncertain, uncomfortable, still-becoming? How might we think about loss as part of the fabric of the quotidian, as a precondition of being together? And what might happen if we think loss in multiple valences, and anticipation in multiple valences, including its ordinary and spectacular iterations, and the multiple forms of harm and possibility it can engender?

Ordinary Letters

My move to Chicago was the very first time that I did not have my eyes on my parents. I was a new parent juggling the relentless demands of a small child. I was a newly tenured professor juggling the relentless demands of a new job. In the three years that I spent in Chicago, I could see—*feel*—my mother receding. By the time I flew from Chicago to New Jersey to accompany my mother to her first visit to a neurologist—a visit I commemorated with a singular photograph, a view of an icy Chicago from the airplane, a picture I sent to my husband from the runway of Midway International Airport with the caption "mistakes were made"—I already knew what the diagnosis was.

I broke from, I moved from, and I realized we could not live that way. I quickly learned that a future of us aging across time zones and flying distances wasn't tenable. It was a time that was saturated with loss: some so large that they are catastrophic—my mother's diagnosis—and some so small that I don't even know how to characterize them except to describe an image: my office perched on the top of a modern building, a view of downtown Chicago and the lake, everything about it promised: *You have made it*. And yet I would also tell myself, *Nothing can happen for me here*.

You know this story. I have already narrated it here. I moved, my parents moved, and we ended up together living in a place none of us ever imagined. But this isn't a story of having been saved. It is a story about my abiding curiosity about all that has already been lost, and all the losses that are incorporated into the present, that sit in the room with me as I write this.

Which brings me to the letter that begins this chapter. My curiosities about my parents have been magnified by the temporality of anticipation. But for me, anticipation is not a time of waiting for a singular event but a longer anticipation of slow decline, loss in slow motion. We all age: my parents age, my daughter ages, I age. These processes that share the same name feel so different. I secure a job that comes with an embarrassingly long title; my daughter learns how to read; my parents' bodies seem to get smaller by the year.[54] This is all aging, all of it is time passing, but some of it reads as accomplishment and some of it feels like diminishment.

And I am confronted with my own desire to know, to have access to something I can no longer simply ask my mother about: *who was she* when she met my father, when she broke from her own parents. (She didn't really break with. She *escaped*, marrying my father a few weeks after her college graduation, telling me once, "It was live with my father or live with your father. I chose the latter.")

There are two things you should know: First, I am struck by my father's precise cursive. I have never—in my forty-two years of living—seen him use this form of writing, except when he elaborately signs his name on a check, a contract, or, in my childhood days, a credit card slip. And, second, you should know that my father can narrate his life through cars: a story about the cars he owned and those that were "company cars," those he drove in his life as a textbook salesman.

This is a letter from April 1973, the spring of my mother's junior year, sixteen months before my parents' wedding. This is a letter that begins with "I miss you very much. So much so I was coming to see you yesterday but I decided not to."

Go on, I think.

And then it turns into a description of the impediments that kept my father from seeing my mother, namely, that he decided to polish his car.

He continues, "I polished the car yesterday. It looks very nice. I also used some ZIF to zif away the dirt on the front. ZIF never fails. I vacuumed the inners too." He reports on applying for a Gulf Oil card and on a book his professor recommended (*Mental Disorders in Urban Areas*), and before he signs off, tells her, "Lakers lost last night 117–109."

This is an account of the banal that lasted nearly fifty years in the archive of a New Jersey basement and that did not travel in a moving truck to North Carolina.

It is something that I imagined would be a love letter, an account of desire intensified by physical distance. It is instead a different kind of love letter, one that is suffused with the details of ordinary life (all life is ordinary life, I remind myself). It is a love letter that I only now understand as a grief object, as a symbol of loss, as I encounter it now, in the archive of everyday life. I come to it wanting to touch the past, to imagine my mother as she once was reading this, to imagine her young, alive, open to the world.

I see it for what it is: a description of my parents as they have always been, deeply committed to the ordinary. I see my father announcing his affection through the mundane. I imagine my mother learning to receive these quotidian details as a measure of love. I see my father as a young man forging some kind of freedom—a car, a gasoline credit card, a small TV on which to watch a game, a girlfriend in college in upstate New York. I imagine my mother as a young woman receiving what could be thought of as a love letter in her mailbox.

I see it for what it is: an archive of my own desire to capture a moment in which I didn't exist, a time I only describe as *before*, a moment in which my mother's life was opening in front of her. I see it for what it is: something that my father never intended would live on, in his forty-two-year-old daughter's hands (not to mention her book, one that he certainly will not read but certainly will buy to satisfy his own archival impulses), or that he thought would live on only in the form of his long conversation with my mother that has centered on the most ordinary, the stuff of life.[55]

I find myself mourning, thinking of whatever it was they felt then for each other and where they are now, where what I see most profoundly is something I would call devotion. My father tends to my mother, albeit in his own idiosyncratic ways. He listens to her repeated questions, and answers her without frustration. He takes her for ice cream. He tells jokes that are unbearably corny but still amuse her. This isn't the kind of romance I sought in the archive, but it is one of a different sort: marked by attention and loyalty.

This study of letters, then, is a desire to think the place of the ordinary in Black life. It is a sustained rumination on Black living that centers the quotidian, in a Black feminist effort to restore the quotidian and the banal, the blearily ordinary, to Black people who still live as symbols of so much—whether pain or deviance, trauma or excess. My wish is for a Black feminist theory that can contend with this object—the letter that survives and its account of love announced through the mundane, encountered decades later in a season of slow loss—as an articulation of Black loss.

4

Picturing Loss

I look at this picture and realize no one on earth will remember who this is—I
am quite literally the only one who still knows. The image is so tenuously bound
to me and me alone in the universe.

PATRICIA J. WILLIAMS, "Gathering the Ghosts"

"Everyone in this photograph is now dead," Christina Sharpe writes in the
captions of the photographs that end the first chapter of her field-defining
book *In the Wake*.[1] An insistence on the ongoing place of the dead in the
present, the here-and-now of what can seem past, is central to the project
of what she terms "wake work" and "defending the dead."[2] For Sharpe, this
work is a form of justice to the past staged in the present and future.

Sharpe describes wake work as a project centered on *writing*. Much of
Sharpe's book is an intentional search for the written form that can "perform
the labor" of care. She reminds her readers, "I am trying to find the language
for this work, find the form for this work. Language and form fracture more
every day. I am trying, too, to find the words that will articulate care and the
words to think what Keguro Macharia calls those 'we formations.' I am trying to think how to perform the labor of them."[3] She reminds Black studies
scholars that we must become "undisciplined," that we must refuse practices

of writing that produce Black "annihilation."[4] If wake work is about language, about articulating "we formations," this chapter takes as a point of departure a curiosity about the status of the photographs that end Sharpe's opening chapter. What work do these images perform? What are they meant to signal or evoke, and what role do they play in helping Sharpe forge an argument about "words that will articulate care"? If wake work is about the search for language, why the primacy of the image?

Everyone in this photograph is now dead.

I think of a framed photograph that ended up on my parents' wall sometime after I left their house for college: a woman whose hair is pulled back tightly into a bun. She clutches three small children. The picture is gray and faded. There is a look of anxiety on all four faces. I had never seen it before, and I was surprised to find it hanging in a place of prominence. My mother's family seemed to have no history. Or perhaps it's that for most of my life, my mother's family seemed sparsely populated. An only child whose mother was an only child, my mother inhabited a small universe. Her father was born in Barbados, and his mother died when he was a small child. That early death—I don't know the year or the circumstances of it—and then his family's move to the United States seemed to have cast him and his siblings into a largely unarchived childhood.

When he began to pursue graduate work in English at Brooklyn College, completing his master's degree, securing employment as a professor at Brooklyn College, and working toward completing his PhD, he began to exist in an official record. There have been moments in my own professional life when tracing his archived professional life has felt of the utmost importance to me. Once, I contacted Brooklyn College and requested copies of recorded interviews I learned that they held. The librarian kindly sent me a package of meticulously labeled CDs—even told me he remembered my grandfather—and when the discs arrived, I heard my grandfather's voice for the first time in over a decade. There he was, speaking about something utterly banal, and I was riveted. The fact of his existence, the fact that he might understand my existence, the fact of our shared institutional lives, fifty years apart. What loss, I thought, and what relief—not just to hear his voice but to *feel* it.

And then there is my mother's mother, the woman whose first name is my middle name, the one whom I know primarily from watching her recede from social life. I remember mostly that the distance between my grandmother and the rest of the world seemed to deepen until she was unreachable, until her dementia was a chasm between her and us. There is also how she is described by doctors when I disclose my family history. She is treated—condemned, really—as a point of origin in a narrative of what is thought of as inherited illness. My doctor circles her name on the paper where I recount my family history of Alzheimer's and tells me that my grandmother is where our family's entanglement with illness begins, at least as far as we know. I am told that I can have a test to detect the presence of a gene that will tell me something about my future. I never give this a second thought. I live with a knowledge of my history; I know the women who have come before me. I have seen what they have lost, and what it has meant to bear those losses for them and the ones they hold closest. I don't need a swab, a smear, or a test to offer an account of what a future of loss might hold. Instead, I refuse a story where my grandmother is narrated as a flawed actor who has contaminated our gene pool. On the days where the future seems to be only about the probability that my own mind will become unfamiliar to me, I do Pilates, I write, I walk. I entertain the fantasy that I can will myself away from a future that may—or may not—await me. On other days, nothing seems more important than recognizing—inhabiting, even—the connections between my body and the bodies of the women who came before me.

When my grandparents died, my mother inherited their brownstone, which is to say she inherited fifty years' worth of stuff. They were people who lived through the Great Depression with a sense that nothing should be wasted—not a sliver of soap, not a twist tie, not a plastic bag. Inheritances are never uncomplicated, and for my mother this one was complicated by the fact that the brownstone had been retrofitted to deal with the combination of my grandmother's Alzheimer's and my grandfather's steadfast commitment to caring for her at home until he couldn't anymore. The ending of their story, and the story of that house, is a tragic one. They were moved to a nursing home a few miles away. The house sat rotting, with their belongings rotting inside. My grandfather would say that he was rotting in the nursing home, where he and my grandmother would die eleven months apart in adjoining rooms. She couldn't remember who he was, who we were, or, the nurse liked to say, who she was, though I like to think—perhaps to fantasize—that she knew precisely who she was, that she had simply become someone different, and that difference was unbearable for us but perhaps, at times (hopefully), tolerable for her. Out of that "maw of oblivion that is the dumpster"—the wreckage of a house that has twice been flipped since my parents sold it—came this recovered object, a photograph: a woman, three children, none of them recognizable to me.[5] *These are our people*, my mother tells me.[6]

Everyone in this photograph is now dead.

It is strange—harrowing, even—to move alongside this faded image of people I do not know and to find myself searching for signs of resemblance. Perhaps, I think, the woman in the center of the photograph has the large forehead that has come to be the hallmark of my face. Perhaps one child's dark eyes resemble my daughter's. But what I am most interested in is the fact of the picture that my mother hangs up to evidence something: life once lived, and a commitment to honoring that life in the present. I see it as proof of a dense set of desires that came to animate my mother's life in the years between her parents' deaths and her own diagnosis, her way of coming to terms with the narrative of being a person without a history and being—as she told me in a moment of surprising vulnerability after her mother died—*an orphan now.*

The photograph is the object that organizes this chapter. I am curious about the object on my parents' wall, curious about what my mother wanted from it and about my own sense that I could not part with it, even as I am puzzled by what it means to feel attached to something that I cannot decipher. In this chapter I think about how the photograph has come to undergird the dominant form of Black feminist writing that this book tracks, curious about the photograph as a representation of Black loss, whether animated by a desire to construct and claim an archive of Black life and death from absence, or underpinned by a wish to "defend the dead." While the photograph is at the center of this chapter, the family photograph takes on particular prominence here because it is an object that stands in as evidence of intimate loss and that allows Black feminist theorists to get close to loss and to demand that their readers get close to losses that they may or may not understand as their own.[7] I study attempts by Black feminist writers to make us *feel* kinship with historical actors, and to consider historical writing and album-making as a process of forging intimate connections with subjects we never knew. At times, authors like Sharpe explicitly draw on their familial photographic archives to explicate the landscape of Black loss. At other times, authors like Saidiya Hartman craft albums to invite some readers to feel historical subjects as kin, encouraging them to forge connections—real or imagined—with the past.[8]

The photograph becomes a kind of emblem of grief, and it is mobilized to make a claim that Black loss can be rendered visible and that this visibility brings us closer to Black loss. This chapter maintains a deep curiosity around the sense that loss and living with loss can be visualized and that this seeing does something—to its reader and to its writer. I am interested in how the photograph both displays the author's proximity to loss, her intimacy with it, and invites the reader into that same intimacy, allowing us to see the faces of those who aren't here.

Everyone in this photograph is now dead.

How do we understand—*feel*—the notion of Black loss differently when we confront the faces of those who are no longer here? What is the demand that this writing makes of us as readers, and how do the practitioners of this form of writing see this demand as an ethic rather than an extraction of affect? What does it mean to want to make Black women's loss seeable, and what do Black feminist writers think visualizing it and allowing others to see it might make possible? Why has it become so important to Black feminist writers that readers see and face loss?

But this proximity to loss is about a kind of complicated temporal dance, an insistence that the dead lived, that the past is present and even part of an imagined future. The photograph, then, indexes the desires and even fantasies that swirl around loss, including longings to touch the past, to have the past and the future touch, to do justice to what has been lost by making it visible, to insist on living on in the face of loss.[9] All of these desires coalesce around an emphasis on being close to loss, being intimate with loss, as an ethical practice and a mode of living *with* and living *on*. I see the value of proximity to loss, the sense that doing justice to it requires being near it and that the picture makes this moving toward loss, sitting with it, possible, as the heart of the contemporary voice of Black feminist theory. Of course, as this book argues again and again, proximity is marked by its own forms of distance, by places of not-knowing, uncertainty, and mystery. I try to think about how the photograph promises us something—and Black feminist writers deploy photographs to promise us something—and reveals to us only what cannot be fully known, what is uncertain, what is ambivalent. In this chapter I think with work by Saidiya Hartman, Patricia J. Williams, Nicole Fleetwood, and Tina Campt to explore what kinds of losses the photograph allows them to represent and what those images are imagined to evidence. I trace their dual desires for enduring proximity to their own losses and their ethical desire to bring readers closer to the scene of loss through photography.

While the presence of the photograph could be interpreted as conveying Black feminists' sense of the limits of the written word itself—the photograph appears as a sign or symbol of what words cannot describe or will not capture—I instead argue that beautiful writing has performed its work through the creation of a Black feminist grammar that is *always* both discursive and visual. Or, to say it another way, contemporary Black feminist writing is visual, and the beautiful writing that is the object of this book is about genre transgression. It is, of course, Black feminist work that has taught us to "listen to images," to think about how the word is both sonic and visual at the same time.[10] Indeed, while the writing that I center in this chapter might be described as genre-bending or genre-breaking, I describe it differently, tracing how the centrality of the photograph to beautiful writing has yielded books that might be described as *albums*, a term that I use to play with its visual and sonic meanings, with the capacity of the album to echo and reverberate across genres. In this chapter I examine how a now dominant form of Black feminist writing has made image circulation and assembly central to the project of writing itself, using the image as a way of making visible not just loss but the living *with* loss. I think through what the picture does alongside my ambivalent relationship to the family photographs I live with, and alongside my ongoing journey to stay close to the person I miss most—my mother—even as she is sitting in this room with me as I write.[11]

Connection

Nicole Fleetwood's work demonstrates how the photograph transports us to the scene of loss, bringing us close—sometimes unbearably close—to what we grieve. Her brilliant work has transformed the study of prison art and carceral aesthetics, examining incarcerated people's production and circulation of art as an abolitionist vision. In an early iteration of what would become her celebrated monograph *Marking Time*, Fleetwood published an article studying how "vernacular photography that takes place in prison circulates as practices of intimacy and attachment between imprisoned people and their loved ones."[12] That article draws on an archive of her family's collection of pictures of incarcerated relatives to examine how photographs document intimacy, care, and tenderness. These photographs are a record of "marking time together" and a practice of staying connected in the context of carceral institutions that explicitly work to regulate and break intimacy.[13] Fleetwood's article begins with a confession:

> In the first few years of Allen's [Fleetwood's cousin] incarceration, I could not look at these pictures that arrived tucked behind his letters. I dreaded opening an envelope from him if I could feel the contents included something akin to the thickness and flexibility of photographic paper. I would quickly glance and put the image back in the

envelope, feeling much more comfortable with his words. With his words, I had space to process and react. With the photograph, I had difficulty controlling my emotions and reactions. Over time, I learned to prepare myself for an onslaught of feelings that always settled into a lingering sadness and sense of helplessness. After a brief and steadied glance, I would store the envelope in the suitcase under my bed.[14]

I begin with Fleetwood's observation that the photograph has a particular affective power that words do not, that the image has a distinct capacity to undo her. Later, Fleetwood emphasizes that she understood Allen's request for photographs as analogous to those of "other populations removed from their loved ones—those in exile or at war, migrant workers, those estranged from their families who stay connected through letter writing and family photographs."[15] I start with Fleetwood's confession, with the arresting affective power of the photograph, and thus with the ways that Black feminist writers mobilize pictures *in their writing*, aspiring also to produce feelings of intimacy and proximity between the reader (who becomes a viewer) and the writer.

One way of living with the image and its affective power, Fleetwood discloses, was to put the photographs under the bed, to tuck them away. But the article traces Fleetwood's transformation in how to live with the photograph when the image is—in and of itself—a repository of loss and grief. She describes an "experiment" where she hung the pictures around her house and "greeted these photos and smiled back at them. After a while, they no longer unsettled me. They were just there, along with all the other possessions and images in my cluttered life."[16] I understand this "experiment" to be an engagement with the question of how to live with loss, how to imagine loss not as spectacular or incidental to the ordinary but as part of the fabric of the everyday. I also take Fleetwood to underscore that the picture brings us close—perhaps unsettlingly close—to the scene of loss in a way that other forms do not, that it offers us evidence of loss in ways that make the pain of absence particularly visible.

The photograph's status as a grief object is something Tina Campt also explores in her investigation of an ethical question: Does a scholar of Black visual culture subject images of her own family to intellectual analysis? Campt ends her book *Image Matters* by describing the evenings following her mother's death, and the changes that loss engendered: days spent home from school, the presence of "mourner-revelers" in her house recounting stories about her mother, and her father listening to Roberta Flack's *Killing Me*

Softly on repeat. As Campt writes, "He [Campt's father] seemed transported by that song. My mom had died, and he was both upbeat and sad. It was clear that he was devastated by this loss. He was overwhelmed by its enormity and was marshaling his strength and the formidable resources of our family to deal with it. But not quite yet, for in the moment he seemed to be giving himself wholly and completely to the glorious Ms. Flack."[17] How can one describe those moments in words? This is precisely the work the image so often performs, an illustration of all that exceeds or troubles language. Isn't this the work that Black feminists ask the image to enact, to offer us an intimate proximity to loss that words are thought to be unable to touch?

But Campt instead concludes the book without including the image—or at least without including all of the images—of her family photographs. Instead, she asks:

> What about my own family photos? Should I have included them here, and if so, could I have read them in the same way as those I have engaged in these pages? My honest answer is that I cannot . . . My wounded relation to my family photos hampers my ability to produce nuanced readings that do justice to their complexity; it hampers my ability to produce readings equivalent to those presented in the preceding chapter. Yet this wounded relation is, at the same time, a powerful demonstration of this book's central argument: that photographs are extremely affective objects.[18]

I cannot.

For Campt, the fact that the images are *not* included in her book reveals their centrality to grief and loss, how they are "extremely affective objects."[19] In other words, the absence of the images is not about advancing a conception of Black privacy, something that has become more profoundly championed in the moment marked by Black studies' turn to refusal, fugitivity, and interiority. Instead, Campt tells us, "There are some moments, some feelings and emotions, and, indeed, some affects that cannot be captured in images and that escape visual capture in the images that we have."[20] There are times the image fails, she tells us, because we presume that it can "capture" affect, that it can offer us an intimacy to feeling that we cannot access otherwise. And yet, in the absence of the image, Campt underscores that the photograph holds a power—persuasive, analytic, affective—that nothing else can. How might we be moved by seeing these pictures, their absence requires us to ask. Their omission from the text almost seems to make the case for their persuasive power, for their capacity to do something to us as readers, even as she insists that she wants to think about their inability to capture feeling.

But my interest here is not in the limit of the image, or in its power to offer a definitive truth when we know that memory—whether in our minds or in a photograph—is always imperfect. Instead, I start with the dilemma that Fleetwood's and Campt's respective texts make visible, as both grapple with the affective life of living with images, and the affective life of living with images of those we hold dearest, particularly those we miss. For Fleetwood, living with images is a practice of living with loss, and for Campt, living *without* the reproduction of the image is a way of living with loss. For both, the question of closeness to loss—whether one that the photograph makes possible or renders impossible—is central to their exploration of the felt life of Black loss.

The Family Album

Like many canonical Black feminist works, Saidiya Hartman's *Wayward Lives, Beautiful Experiments* defies categorization.[21] In her narration of the book's refusal of categories and genre, Hartman notes, "The book has had a very complex reception. I've been exploring the same set of critical questions since the beginning. But some people in the university world are, like, *Scenes of Subjection* [Hartman's first book] is the real thing. What are these other two books?"[22] She goes on to describe how many have told her, "I like that novel," and confesses, "I'm so unfaithful to genre, so it was fine."[23] The same article reports that her British publisher, Profile Books, classified *Wayward Lives* as both literature and history (in the US, *Wayward Lives* was awarded the National Book Critics Circle award for criticism, not nonfiction); it cut the endnotes that marked the US edition, "allowing the book to be read as creative nonfiction rather than as scholarship."[24] I am interested in *Wayward Lives'* ability not to upend genre but to entirely elude it, because the text refuses to conform to the standards of any prescribed form. One can't help but ask: What *is* this book?

Wayward Lives' unwillingness to be categorized, and Hartman's infidelity to genre, is at least in part because of the book's status as an album, its insistence on incorporating the photograph into the text. The *New Yorker* describes the visual logics of the book, calling Hartman a "filmmaker, pulling back the lens to reveal characters at the margins of the frame."[25] The notion of Hartman as filmmaker suggests that she is working with footage—splicing, arranging, and cutting—that her conception of historical writing is rooted in a visual project, that part of her project of documenting Black women's waywardness and its world-making possibilities is ensuring her readers can envision it. How can we *see* the past, particularly pasts that have been lost, erased, willfully forgotten, or wholly pathologized? Why is *seeing* lost pasts so necessary for claiming them, for imagining them, for getting close to them? What does *seeing* the past do to ameliorate or repair loss?

Building on her methodologically innovative practice of "critical fabulation," *Wayward Lives* offers an account and a "re-creation" of the "radical imagination and wayward practices of young black women in the early 20th century, from about 1890 to 1935."[26] Hartman's intellectual project can be thought of as a long engagement with ideas of Black loss: what has been lost to the discipline of history; what the discipline of history has lost; what "violence . . . deposited" Black life into the archive; what it means to recover, restore, or reimagine when recovery is always ever only partial and illusory; and what it means to write Black living into archives that have centered Black death and loss.[27] Hartman asks, "What are the kinds of stories to be told by those and about those who live in such an intimate relationship with death? Romance? Tragedies? . . . How does one revisit the scene of subjection without replicating the grammar of violence?"[28] These are questions about the ethics of representing Black loss and about the desires to offer an account that does not replicate the violence of the archive itself, that can hold loss in its multifacetedness. But *Wayward Lives* takes up loss differently, by returning to the scene of loss, to the face of those who have been lost, by reproducing the image. If critical fabulation seemed to be a project about writing differently, and particularly a commitment to the speculative and the subjunctive, here I contend that Hartman's work has also been marked by an investment in the visual, making the past seeable.

Wayward Lives is a scrapbook, a collage, a "dream book for existing otherwise," and, as Hartman calls it, "an album."[29] And it is a particular kind of album, one that looks and feels like a family album. With her insistence on uncaptioned images and even on including images that are left unexplicated in the text, Hartman offers her reader photographs of historical actors whose lives she imagines and re-archives, whose ordinary practices of rebellious living she celebrates. In presenting their quotidian practices of living on the intimate scale of the album—Black women dancing, eating, posing, lounging at the beach, talking with friends—her readers are invited to see these women and girls not as removed historical actors but as kin, as *our people*. I see this act of "intimate history" as an invitation that the Black women whose lives she both meticulously and creatively archives—women who were lost to conventional archives and historical narratives that could not see their ordinary practices of pleasure as forms of Black life—can be claimed by readers.[30] Here I mean *claiming* not in the sense of the exertion of a propertied conception of ownership nor as a kind of capture. Instead, I mean it as in *identification*; as Hartman writes elsewhere, the capacity "to see her, yet not reproduce the violence of the compelled image, but instead cloak her in the collective utterance, take on the labor of care, form a circle around her."[31] This ability to "see her" and to "take on the labor of care," to "form a circle around her," is made possible, at least in part, by the book's preoccupation with the photograph. Of course, identification is complicated terrain, some of which is mapped in the previous chapter when I think about the Black epistolary tradition and the question of audience. But I treat the visual component of Hartman's historiographical effort as an invitation to closeness, to encounter historical actors in the context of an intimate archive that *feels* different from what a reader might anticipate. Hartman has expressed her desire to offer the image not in the service of the sociological but instead in the hopes of documenting beauty. She notes, "These photographs never grasped the beautiful struggle to survive, glimpsed the alternative modes of life, or illuminated the mutual aid and communal wealth of the slum. The reform pictures and the sociological surveys documented only ugliness. Everything good and decent stood on the ruins of proscribed modes of affiliation and ways of living: the love unrecognized by the law, households open to strangers, the public intimacy of the streets, and the aesthetic predilections and willful excesses of young black folks."[32] But she takes the images and underscores the "struggle to survive" as an act and practice of beauty, as a "willful" insistence on life and living. This is the political and ethical work of history writing as album-making: it is the task of encouraging readers to imagine what Jennifer Morgan described as the feeling of "kinfulness," finding and forging the feeling of kin with those no longer here, with those who have been lost to conventional archives.[33]

In other spaces, I have argued that beauty is at the heart of Hartman's project of "re-creation."[34] I have insisted that Hartman's celebration of Black women and "ordinary colored girls," and her reading of their practices of living, breathing, dancing, walking through the city, gossiping, and sitting in the sand on a hot day, centers beauty as the heart of Black women's living. Hartman writes:

It is hard to explain what's beautiful about a rather ordinary colored girl, a face difficult to discern in the crowd, an average chorine not destined to be a star or even the heroine of a feminist plot. In some regard, it is to recognize the obvious that is reluctantly ceded: the beauty of the black ordinary, the beauty that resides in and animates the determination to live free. Beauty is not a luxury; it is a way of creating possibility in the space of enclosure, a radical art of subsistence, a transfiguration of the given. Only the wayward appreciated this girl's riotous conduct and wild habits—her longing to create a life from nothing. Only they could discern the beautiful plot against the plantation that she waged each and every day.[35]

The *beautiful* plot, the *beautiful* ordinary colored girl, *beauty* as an act of subsistence, *beauty* as possibility.

Hartman insists not just that "a rather ordinary colored girl" should be an object of study but also that key to understanding her commitment to the "wild habit" of living is reading her life as a commitment to beauty. Beauty is a practice, Hartman tells us, an orientation toward living, and a belief in the possibility and practice of "creat[ing] a life from nothing."[36] Crafting an "album" of ordinary colored girls requires a reading practice attuned to how Black women forged beauty not as "a luxury" but as a mode of everyday life. To be clear, this is a fundamental reconception of what beauty looks like, looking not for signs of luxury, excess, or indulgence, nor for beauty as pedagogical, but instead for the aesthetics of the ordinary, for what Sharpe describes as

> a list on a slip of paper in a book
> the arrangement of pins in cloth
> the ability to make firewood out of newspaper.[37]

But Hartman also insists that the way to describe Black women's commitment to beauty is to write differently, to write beautifully. This is a kind of writing that echoes the forms of living she wants to chart. She opens the book with a description of her method, the only moment in the book that adheres to the norms of academic writing. She tells her reader that she has had to "make use of a vast range of archival materials to represent the everyday experience and restless character of life in the city."[38] Her desire is "to exhume open rebellion from the case file" to offer an account of the "everyday anarchy of ordinary colored girls."[39] As Hartman tells us, her primary method is to "press at the limits" of the case file, to "imagine," to "speculate," and she describes her book as an "album" that is an "archive of the exorbitant, a dream book for existing otherwise."[40] This "pressing," "exhuming," "speculating," and "imagining" requires Hartman to deploy a form of writing that is lyrical and poetic, attentive to the smallest details of ordinary life. In arguing that beauty is as necessary as breathing, she writes with a careful, thoughtful attention to the smell of spring possibility on a city corner, the quick touch of fingers rubbing against each other, the gesture, the look, the hint, the touch.

The result of this method of "pressing," "imagining," and "exhuming" is a writing that is hybrid. It is not simply that it crosses or even refuses genre. It produces an intimacy through its juxtaposition of text and image, particularly its inclusion of photographs that appear without caption or explication. The photographs' captions are included at the very end of the book in the notes, which demands a certain amount of labor on the part of the reader. In fact, the placement of the captions at the end of the book invites the reader to *not* read them, to encounter the photographs and to imagine the stories of those represented. Thus, the book not only documents "open rebellion" and "everyday anarchy" but also suggests that we get close to it through engaging its practitioners intimately, by looking closely at their faces, by encountering them in a form that feels like a family album. In describing the book as a family album, I do so fully aware of all the complex circuits of feelings that the family album can produce. Albums can produce recognition and misrecognition; we can think we see our own faces in the images; we can bear the shock of not seeing our own faces. They can produce tenderness, rage, ambivalence, and a host of other feelings. They often—though not always—invite us to think, as Patricia J. Williams does, "It brings felt meaning to the koan that novelist and Zen master Ruth Ozeki frequently cites as her meditative inspiration: 'What did your face look like before your parents were born?'"[41] In other words, these are affectively saturated objects dense with historical desires, spaces where the present, past, and future touch.

One of the images that accompanies Hartman's "The Beauty of the Chorus" is of two women standing on the beach. There are two houses behind them; in the distance, a few other figures are lounging in the sand. One woman wraps her arms around the other in a tight embrace. Their feet are buried in the sand. They are smiling brightly. They are bent forward toward the camera. Their skin is glazed by the sun. It is a scene of joyful tenderness that captures friendship and the sheer pleasure of a summer afternoon spent on the beach where there is nothing guiding the day except for leisure and the prospect of time spent together. I have no idea who they are, how they know each other (though I feel certain by their physical closeness and ease, by the tightness of the embrace, that they do in fact know each other well).[42] If I turn to the captions at the back of the book, I learn that this image is from the Pauli Murray collection and that these are, as the caption says, "two women hugging." But when I encounter them in the book, with no caption to narrate the image, I am struck more than anything by the delight they seem to take in sun, in sand, in relaxation. I savor how their bodies become illustrations of Hartman's idea of "the chorus" even as I can encounter them with little idea of who they were, what chorus they were a part of, and when they engaged in their radical acts of assembly.

A few pages later, I see another Black woman on the beach. She is reclining in the sand. There are beach umbrellas around her, and I can view the legs of whoever is accompanying her, a woman whose head is cut off by the edge of the photograph. But I can see that she lounges on her stomach, I can see her bare legs stretched long, and I see the face of a smiling woman who is enjoying a hot summer day at the beach. This image, I learn, is titled *On the Beach*, and it is from the Mabel Hampton Collection at the Lesbian Herstory Archives (which has myriad images of Hampton and her friends at the beach). Hampton is a central figure in Hartman's description of the "beauty of the chorus," someone whom Hartman describes as "ach[ing] for something better, for an arena other than the kitchen or bedroom for the display of her capacities and talents."[43] But for Hartman, it is Hampton at the beach that allows us to see something particular about Black women's living. The beach, Hartman reminds her readers, is a place of play and eroticism, of flesh and sun; it is a place where "limbs [are] sticky and entwined, . . . bodies barely within the legal limit of decency. . . . People poured into Coney Island from all over New York to make love on the beach. . . . All along the beach people had intercourse. It was as much a wonder as the ocean."[44] We encounter these images embedded in text; the text around them is an explication, an illustration, though as readers, we never know if the figures who appear in the photographs are the ones that Hartman describes. Whether the album invites readers to see the women represented as their own people, as kin, is another question. But it is certainly the case that part of the workings of intimate history is a relationship to loss that invites readers not simply to recover but to imagine the feeling of sand on toes, the possibility in the spring air, the hum of the city even in the middle of the night, and what all of these things felt like for the women who appear on the page, not just in description but in image.

If much of *Wayward Lives* offers its reader the intimacy of a family photo album, inviting us to visualize the narratives that surround the photographed subjects, or to work to understand how they correspond to the narratives Hartman offers, how the pictures align with the text to produce a scrapbook that captures a life lived, the book ends with a surprising picture. Hartman's book closes with a celebration of the chorus, which "makes a plan, they draft a blueprint: move, escape, rush to the city, quit the job, and run away from everything hellbent on sucking all the life out of them."[45] For Hartman, these "blueprints" are pathways to freedom; they are about movement—away from the job, toward forms of friendship, against captivity. There is motion, energy, activity, all oriented toward freedom in the space of the enclosure. Hartman writes, "The Greek etymology of the word *chorus* refers to *dance within an enclosure*. What better articulates the long history of struggle, the ceaseless practice of Black radicalism and refusal, the tumult and upheaval of open rebellion than the acts of collaboration and improvisation that unfold within the space of enclosure?"[46]

And in a book of images of Black women's freedom, their everyday acts of living and being together, Hartman closes with yet another photograph. But this one is not an image of women on the beach, dancing, or sitting together. It is a picture of a flock of birds flying in formation. Hartman writes, "The collective movement points toward what awaits us, what has yet to come into view, what they anticipate—the time and place better than here, a glimpse of the earth not owned by anyone. . . . Inside the circle it is clear that every song is really the same song, but crooned in infinite variety, every story altered, and unchanging: *How can I live? I want to be free. Hold on.*"[47] That question "How can I live?" is illustrated with the stunning synchronized choreography of birds traveling collectively in an organized group. The image is photographed by Swiss photographer Lukas Felzmann, who has devoted his work to studying the patterns and formations of flight, and the mystical and mysterious crossings of birds across the sky. Felzmann's images pulse with the vibrancy of motion, even as we—the viewers—have no idea what these birds are moving toward, or away from, only that they are in motion.[48]

How might we understand the decision to end *Wayward Lives* with an image where "no one bears the burden alone of figuring out the next move"?[49] Perhaps this photograph suggests that some things can't be represented in human forms, that imagining freedom requires a combination of mystery, poetry, and abstraction. Perhaps this image emphasizes that freedom is a form of anti-captivity that privileges a collective movement *toward* something. And perhaps this photograph centers the necessary blurring between the individual and the collective in any vision of freedom dreaming. Perhaps what Hartman leaves us with is a call for a desire for flight as where an intimate history begins and ends, even if it leaves us away from the bodies of the women who animate this text.

In the Company of Ghosts

Patricia J. Williams's "Gathering the Ghosts" is a rumination on the status of the photograph for Black intimate histories. The essay begins by describing an issue of *Radcliffe Magazine* that featured a photograph of Williams cradling a picture of her mother. As she recounts it, "Quite unexpectedly, this innocuous image brought me literally face to face with many of the ethical dilemmas at the center of a project archiving memories. It was surely very meaningful that my family's collection was so honored. But having my heavily made-up face dispersed to Radcliffe's far-flung readership brought with it a peculiarly personal sense of disembodiment. It was 'me' but it was not 'I.' And the picture I was holding is my late mother, but my mother was younger than I."[50] Her placement on the magazine cover was an institutional celebration of Williams's commitment to archiving her family's photographs and letters at the Schlesinger Library, but it also prompted her to think about "the emotional layers at stake in the constitution of an archive" and the capacity of the image to "quicken the dead and freeze-frame all life."[51] The questions of the ethics of the photograph, the afterlives of images, and the place of Black women as cover girls for institutional projects have long circulated in Williams's work. But here the rumination is on the photograph and its archival travels, its capacity to stand as an index of loss, forgetting, and remembering housed in the cool confines of a university archive.

What does it mean for someone who describes their own life as one marked by histories of being the "object of property" to make property of the past, to insert it into institutional holdings?[52] This is where Williams begins: with her desire to preserve the past and a reckoning with the fact that this preservationist impulse means that her history, stories, and past will be held and handled in myriad ways. This impulse toward preservation, toward being a steward of the past, also renders the past a kind of property that can be accessed and analyzed, that is held, sorted, and curated by an elite private institution that recounts its archival holdings as evidence of its excellence. At one moment, she reflects on how her cover shot felt "intimate and public" and how strange it was to, one night, see a "homeless man in Harvard Square, who was patching his cardboard tent with this [magazine] cover. My glossily airbrushed face was subsumed into the paper's body, weight, texture, and durability. The substantiality of its high-grade bond put my life in context: the utility of my face as curtain, my persona a decorative detail."[53] Williams attends to the lives and afterlives of property, and Black women's complicated entanglements with becoming property, making property, ownership, and dispossession.

But for Williams, the photograph is a particular kind of archival object. It stands as evidence of what was here before, *who* was here before. It is a remedy for loss, an insistence on making the "ghosts" into people with specific and recounted histories. It points to lives lived, and the loss of those lives now. As she writes, "I yearn to have future beings see me and my wonderful forefathers and mothers. *We were all here!*"[54]

We were all here!

There is something about "seeing" that she dreams will allow "future beings" to know that some past beings were here. The image is proof of life. And, for Williams, the image is also a way of thinking about—and with—lives that were shaped by violence, histories that were constituted by erasure. While the photograph cannot repair, it does *something* for Williams to do justice to a past marked by dispossession. Williams returns to her great-great-grandmother Sophie, who animates much of her thinking in *The Alchemy of Race and Rights*. As she writes:

> I grew up living in the past: the future, some versions of which only had the vaguest possibility of happening, was treated with the respect of the already-happened, seen through the prismatic lenses of what had already occurred. Thus, when I decided to go to law school my mother told me that "the Millers were lawyers so you have it in your blood." (Of course Mother did not mean that law was literally part of my genetic makeup; she meant that law was an intimate part of the socially constructed reality into which I had been born. . . .
>
> [T]he Millers were the slaveholders of my maternal grandmother's clan. The Millers were also my great-great grandparents and great-aunts and who knows what else. My great-great grandfather Austin Miller, a thirty five year old lawyer, impregnated my eleven year old great great

grandmother Sophie . . . In ironic, perverse obeisance to the rational-
izations of this bitter ancestral mix, the image of this self-centered
child molester became the fuel for my survival in the dispossessed
limbo of my years at Harvard.[55]

It is Austin Miller's story and Sophie's, the "interplay of notions of public
and private, of family and market; of male and female, of molestation and
the law" that animates what Williams calls her search for "her shape and his
hand."[56] This search is more than method or reading practice; it is an ethic
and a way of living, an insistence on attending to what Avery Gordon will
call "ghostly matters." But for Williams, Sophie exists without an image. She
cannot picture her. Williams writes, "I mourn not having pictures of her. I
mourn her. I am committed to rendering her into existence, to make a mark
on her behalf, to give her form and face, to cherish her in the not-national
archive of my memory. And so I dream her, but she is unthinkable."[57] There
is something about the absence of a picture that makes "rendering her into
existence" a different kind of challenge (as if the image would be proof of her
existence). To think her without the photograph requires Williams to "dream
her." This is the affective and political currency the picture holds for Williams.

But what happens when the photograph—itself an archive of loss—has
no one to narrate it, to explain it, to offer a caption, informal or formal? As
Williams anxiously writes, "I hand over these pictures of the past as a gift to
the future. But so much needs translation."[58] The act of gathering the ghosts
is made possible through the image, and yet as she warns, "The archive is filled
with questions and unidentified faces."[59] We do not live on, even when the
photograph does. Williams suggests that much of her own work is animated
by a desire—however futile—to find the right way to frame these images so
that they can live "correctly" in the absence of someone to explain them. As
she says, "I wish them to live in social imagination more fully than many of
them were able to while on the planet. And so I need to explain. I am constantly explaining. I am always looking for the right words, the right accent,
the perfect analogy, the smoothest homology, the felt connection, the link that
sparks a mental orgasm of humanizing recognition. I throw myself at this task
over and over again. It's promethean. It's obsessive, compulsive, disordering.
But I also like to think of it as principled folly, moral insistence, an endeavor
for the long haul."[60] Of course the idea of the caption, the framing, the narrative as providing a "right" way to read the past—or even a way that does
justice to the complexity of the historical actors we claim as our people—is

its own fiction, but I take from Williams both the desire that the image live on and the risk that the image poses. Yet Williams emphasizes that this is a risk worth taking, that the photograph gives us—in the present—a way of seeing and even touching the past, a way of incorporating dispossession into selfhood and thus finding a way to "own the self in a disowned world," or, as Williams says, "Claiming for myself a heritage the weft of whose genesis is my own disinheritance is a profoundly troubling paradox."[61]

My People

I have moved a lot. I have lived in Cambridge, Massachusetts (twice); New York City; Washington, DC; Chicago; and Durham, North Carolina, all in the span of thirteen years. As I mentioned in the book's preface, these moves have all been in the service of my professional life and the promise of stability and intellectual freedom. If anything, my life as an academic has trained me to become an expert in assembling and unpacking my belongings, making and unmaking a life. I have become adept at fitting my life into the number of boxes that can comfortably fit into a mover's truck.

But in any place I—we, actually (here, reader, I should mention that I have a husband, who is a writer, and we have always had a pact that we don't write about each other. This has been perhaps because of some shared sense of privacy and some sense that there are things we simply don't mine on the page. I am not sure if this is a violation of the pact, but I feel that to write him out of this story would be its own act of infidelity)—have called home, we have hung up a wall of photographs. In the earliest days of our life together, the wall of photographs was an attempt to represent that our lives had merged. Across age, geography, race, and time, we had intentionally produced a life together. The act of making and merging lives was not without loss, especially for him. We have become outsiders to his family as we made our life together. Sometime over the past twenty years, we realized we could either contort ourselves to fit comfortably inside the parameters of an intimate world that could not truly see us, or we could make our own world. We chose the latter.

Now we have a daughter. Her childhood has been, in many ways, out of time. She is sixteen years younger than my stepson and twelve years younger than her youngest cousins. She is far from my husband's family in India, which, for her, has become a place that exists in stories and photographs. It is a place she hears—because you can *hear* India on the phone—when she calls her grandparents. But it is not a place she has visited. The wall of photographs has been a visual reminder that she comes from someplace, that she has a people. I see her squint at the figures in the frames as we tell her stories: *These are your people.*

The wall is an archive of so many losses—in the time that we have been together, my father-in-law died. His was a COVID death, even though he didn't die of COVID. But dying during pandemic time meant that no one was there to mourn him; instead, we did it on Zoom, and grief became pixelated, and the strange asynchronicity meant someone was always talking over someone else. Sentences were started and then abandoned and then ran into each other. My daughter doesn't remember her grandfather. Instead, she remembers stories about him, which, for her, have taken the shape of actual memories. And she sees his face on the wall and will even greet it: *There's Dada looking young.* There is a picture from our wedding, and with each passing year, I note the distance between how young and unlined our faces were then and how much we have transformed. It is hard to describe the subtle ways our bodies have changed as the years pass: some parts have softened, others have hardened; there is still the kernel of the people who assembled on the steps of a small chapel in Cambridge, Massachusetts, but so much has been remade.

There is a picture of my parents on that wall, right next to the picture of my father-in-law. It was taken at some point in the early years of their relationship, probably at Vassar College. It is black and white, and my parents are standing with their backs to each other. My father's large, round afro fills most of the frame, his face framed by the sideburns that were his signature feature for most of the 1970s. My mother's frizzy hair fills the remaining third of the frame. They look in opposite directions, which, for many years, I took as the perfect metaphor for their marriage: two people bound together by the frame of history, often pulling in different directions. My daughter sees this image as a testament to love: here they are, nearly fifty years later, still bound to each other. I see this image as a testament to loss. There was no sign then of where we would be now. This is true, I suppose, of any image, which captures only the present and is overlaid with the interpretative frame the viewer brings to the image, full of desires and questions.

I rehearse this here to name my own affective attachment to the image, my own desire to script a history for my daughter, to let her know that she has a people *and* that she can decide how to claim those people (and learn if those people will claim her in return). And my own desire to remember my mother as she was, and even as she is, as she is *right now*. I want an image that captures who she is when she is still recognizable to me and while I am still

Naima Ahmad Nash, Jennifer C. Nash, and Carolyn Eastmond Nash
(Photo courtesy of Amin Ahmad)

recognizable to her. I write this sentence realizing that she is in a period of profound transformation. She is becoming someone I don't entirely know, and part of my challenge is to learn to know this new person, to honor the parts of her that still seem familiar, and to acquaint myself with the parts that have emerged and that surprise me. It is laborious and disorienting.

There is one picture that is not on our wall yet. I treasure it and also find it unbearable to live with. In the early days of the pandemic, when my sabbatical had abruptly ended and my daughter's school had closed, we spent weeks just walking anxiously around Cambridge. One afternoon, my parents drove from New Jersey to meet us. There was nowhere to go and nothing to do, but there was the exhilaration of seeing each other, the joy in the break from our routine of simply passing time. My husband had become preoccupied with taking pictures, a way of seeing the world apart from its bleak monotony. The streets were eerily empty, so he would photograph door frames, graffiti, clouds. And then he decided to take pictures of our family. So there is this one—my mother, my daughter, and I are sitting on a bed. We are each consumed by our distinct thoughts. We are bound to each other by threads of history that we each sense differently. We are three generations of women—in the room, at least for me, is a fourth: my grandmother. This picture is now three years old. My daughter is a half foot taller. Her hair has grown long. She is usually carrying a small bag filled with books and pens. I have been aged by the demands of my job, by juggling the care of a still-small child and aging parents. Sometimes I think that there is a permanent look of tiredness imprinted on my face. And my mother, there is something about her face that has changed. There is a sense that she is not quite with us as she was the day this photograph was taken. But that's something I can't put into words; it's only something I can see in the picture.

Conclusion

NEW FURNITURE, OR ALL ABOUT
BLACK FEMINIST THEORY'S FATHERS

What comes after loss?

JOSÉ ESTEBAN MUÑOZ, "Vitalism's After-Burn"

My father is notoriously frugal. He only buys things on sale. He will drive an extra ten minutes to save a fraction of a dollar on gasoline. He has had the same brown plastic coupon box for as long as I can remember, and he displays his affection by arriving at my house and asking, "Quilted Northern? Do you use that? There's a good coupon here!" There is a longer story about his own histories of loss: my father began his working life at fourteen while his father recovered from a rare jaw cancer. He sewed zippers onto handbags, swept the floors of an ice cream shop, sorted mail in corporate law firm offices at night. He has known kinds of work that I have never experienced; sometimes I think he has organized his entire life to spare me from the kinds of work he has known. I know that his frugality comes from a sense that things can turn on a dime.

But when he and my mother move into a sleek condo in Chapel Hill, North Carolina, he decides he wants new furniture. He asks us to go to Crate and Barrel and to buy everything we can: rugs, lamps, an oversized sectional. He says he wants something "upscale and elegant," and as he repeats this phrase, he makes an expansive gesture with his arms. I am puzzled. My father has always been unwavering in his commitment to self-denial. But suddenly he wants to be surrounded by newness: lush fabrics, bright rugs, curved sofas. He wants comfort, luxury even, and he is committed to reimagining his surroundings. As the weeks go by, the furniture deliveries begin; I walk into my parents' apartment and find them sitting in front of a sleek flat-screen television on an oversized custom-made plush sofa. It feels strange to see them, in their same clothes, with their same habits, suddenly surrounded by newness.

When I finally ask my father what is motivating his desire for new furniture, he confesses: he has started to imagine a life without my mother, or, perhaps more accurately, a life where he can't care for her at home. He realizes that the only way he can manage a future that is not yet here but seems inevitable is to find himself in the company of objects that have no history, that do not remind him of the more than fifty years of living together that they have shared. There is something about the corporate comfortable anonymity of his new furniture that allows him to begin to imagine an unbearable future.

The truth is she is far from this. Or I think she is far from it. There are moments—weeks, even—when I tell myself, *Things are getting better*. I allow myself to forget the future that seems to have been announced in the moment of her diagnosis. I have learned to live around the repeated questions, the times when she forgets the name of a familiar object: *I want that thing you eat with. A fork? Yes, yes, a fork.* There are other moments—weeks, even—when it is so abundantly clear that we have entered some new phase of living with Alzheimer's, that our lives have become both painfully medicalized and curiously unmedicalized (I still remain astounded by the cruelty of the diagnostic moment: "You have Alzheimer's. There's nothing we can do.").

I begin this conclusion with my father. I begin—and end—with him because everything I have learned about devotion has come from watching him care for my mother with gentleness, patience, respect, and a deep affection for their shared history and the life they continue to forge even when it is not the one that either of them expected. If there are frustrations, regrets, or even anger, I see no hints of them. I see only a daily practice of life-making, an "ordinary note of care" in the face of proliferating forgettings, a commitment to strategizing how to keep living a life that matters to them as they contend with the multiplying challenges of the ordinary.[1]

Following Lauren Berlant and Michael Warner's oft-quoted question, "What can queer theory teach us about X?" I remain interested in what—or *how*—Black feminism can teach me.[2] This is what keeps me rooted in the work that I do: a longing to continue to learn from the theoretical tradition that is my intellectual home. Over the course of writing this book, I have found that I am as interested in what Black feminism can teach me about any number of questions as the moments when I realize—or sense—that Black feminism has not yet equipped me to think about a set of questions or objects. Black feminism has taught me so much about mothers and mother-loss, about maternal flesh and maternal metaphors, about maternity and maternal politics. But I do not know how to use the tradition I live with to think about my father. I cannot yet think about the work that he takes on using the theoretical tools I am trained in. This is work that he was not socialized to perform thanks to the highly structured gendered and sexual norms that organized his childhood. This is work that the gendered arrangements of my parents' own marriage spared my father from. This is work that is now his.

The tools that I have to think about the Black family are multiple: decades of Black feminist critiques of the Moynihan Report and its afterlives; scholarly work on the queerness of Black kin and sociality; on Black masculinities; on Black gender, ungendering and re-gendering; and powerful Black feminist critiques of Black patriarchy and popular and scholarly work on the heteronormative Black family as the linchpin of racial progress (and, I admit, some surprising celebrations of Black patriarchy and heteronormativity). But what about the figure of the Black paternal? How might we think about Black fathers—who have for so long been either wholly absent from the Black feminist archive, appearing as a figure of violence, of pathology, of absence, or—in its flip—a figure of resilience? And how do we think about the losses they bear?[3] Or why must loss wear the face of Black mothers for the Black feminist theoretical archive to register it as such?

In asking these questions, I am not amplifying a call to center Black male pain when so much of the grammar of US political life continues to be about dead or dying Black boys and men, and when Black male pain has long overdetermined conversations about Black social life and anti-Blackness. Nor is it a plea to decenter Black mothers even as I remain critical of how Black maternal flesh has become a commodity in a political moment where to name Black mothers' suffering—real or imagined—is thought to be constitutive of a political act. This is also not a call about Black fathers that intends to think solely within a framework of the heterosexual nuclear family, that considers Black fathers only through logics of heteronormativity.

It is instead a query about the figure of the Black paternal *for* the Black feminist theoretical archive, underpinned by an investment in thinking about the variety of paternal figures that provide tenderness and attention. This is a call to think about the multiplicity of paternal figures who bear witness to the ordinariness of slow loss and who offer it companionship through small gestures of everyday tenderness. It is a question that I pose in a long moment when everything I know about commitment comes from watching my father care for my mother. I want to know how I can mobilize Black feminist theory to think with his pain and his love, his labor and his devotion, the ways he lives to help my mother live on and the ways he helps me remember her as she was and love her as she is transforming.

While much of Black studies scholarship has valorized care as a mode of collective survival, I want to mark something different here: tenderness. By *tenderness*, I describe what it means to move with gentleness and affection, care and attention. I also use the word *tenderness* to capture the feeling of being sensitized, open to the world—including to the pain of the world—and vulnerable. I mark the dull ache and the exhaustion that can accompany the repeated work of caregiving, and the feeling of rawness and openness to being moved that can accompany that work. I note the surprise of inhabiting roles that never belonged to us before, the ways that my father now carries on familial labor that once belonged to my mother.

Let me be specific: For years, my mother was the person in charge of gift giving. She would buy holiday presents and birthday presents, elaborately gift-wrap boxes, and tie curlicued ribbons around them. Now, my mother doesn't remember birthdays—hers or ours—and the role of procuring presents, or at least remembering occasions, falls on my father, who will now show up with a Hallmark card he has picked out at Walgreens and a message he has scrawled inside. I sense the awkwardness he feels in inhabiting a role that was never his, and perhaps an awkwardness he feels about gift giving when he didn't grow up giving or receiving them. I sense that he feels an obligation to offer a present, a sadness that a task that had once been my mother's has become his own, and a regret that he is unable to perform it with the joy she used to show. I find myself mourning our old roles—particularly the pleasure my mother took in celebrating birthdays—and in awe of what we have made in this moment in the unfolding present.

Or another example: For years, my mother was the person I would call with health questions. Last year, when my doctor sent me for a follow-up for a routine mammogram, telling me I had "dense breasts" that needed further evaluation, it was my father I called. *Dad, did Mom ever have this?* I ask him. He clears his throat. *Yes, that happened to Mom. Same thing, she went, and they sent her for a follow-up, and it was fine. Call me when you have news.* I text my father after my next mammogram: *All clear.* He sends back a thumbs-up emoji. Neither of us anticipated this conversation, or a few weeks later, when he finds a small lump on his chest and calls me into the bathroom to lift his shirt. *I would ask Mom,* his voice drifts off. I help him raise his shirt, I look at his chest, I press my finger to the place that is tender, I reassure him.

This necessary labor, alongside the persistence of love, has broken my parents' old and tired gendered division of labor, or at least disrupted it. I have seen my father scrub his grandmother's back and comb his mother's hair with a tenderness that shocked me. And I have now seen him do both for my own mother. I write these sentences not out of a desire to champion cisgender heterosexual men who perform the repetitive, ordinary, and essential work of care; these celebrations are, of course, a central way that misogyny operates. Instead, in this conclusion, I mark my curiosity about the figure of the Black paternal, who continues to enter the Black feminist archive primarily as an apparition, and my desire to construct a theoretical apparatus that can help me understand this figure with the complexity the paternal should be afforded.

More than anything, I wonder what Black feminist theory might tell me beyond *care*—a word that has become the centerpiece of not just Black feminist theory but Black studies in the past decade, animating calls for how we might think, live, and love together outside of institutions. I am curious about devotion and tenderness. I want to think about what it means to attend to other people's bodies—scrub their back, comb their hair, wash their hands—and to be made tender, raw even, by that work, particularly when the body that is scrubbed, the hair that is combed, the hands that are washed are those of your Beloved. I endeavor to mobilize Black feminist theory to mark what it feels like to find oneself open, soft, receptive, vulnerable, broken open by love, by fatigue, by repetition, by devotion. I have no answers to these questions, only a desire to underline a place where a Black feminist theoretical tradition is still silent. And I have my own desire to mark my wish to think about how we might begin to craft a theory of devotion, and yes, of beauty, that can think about and beyond the figure of the Black mother, that can think about the myriad forms that the tender act of Black living with loss takes on.

This book began with a series of questions: What does Black feminism have to tell us about loss that unfolds in slow motion—or at least the slow inching toward something we imagine as an ending, a break, a threshold? How can Black feminism narrate forms of loss, grief, and losing that are not sudden and expected but gradual, unfolding, durational? How might Black feminism explain moments that feel like endings but aren't, the ways that loss often unfolds in anti-linear ways? How might it help us understand how slow loss upends time? How might it analyze how loss rewrites histories, how loss becomes a site where memories are written and rewritten? I pose these questions in a moment when, as I argue throughout this book, Black feminism has advanced a singular theory of Black loss that has become highly visible: Black loss is constituted by the sudden—but not unexpected—murder of Black people, particularly Black boys and men, by the state. Black loss is felt and manifested in non-indictments, non-redress, and the invisibility of Black pain to the juridical, even as the cultural is saturated with images of Black pain. Black loss is embodied by Black mothers who are icons of grief and who become the embodiment of Black pain. The widely circulating narrative of Black motherhood is that it is marked by a temporality of anticipation, of loss that is expected, that cannot be guarded against. This is a narrative that has performed its work against the spectacular visibility of Black death—it is screened on phones, as so many writers note, lived with intimately, and also invisible to the state, which continues to raze its existence, or at least to treat it as within the purview of the legal system. There is an ethics to this theory, and a politics as well; there is a desire to respond to anti-Black violence with an insistence on the overwhelmingness of Black grief, on the everydayness and "compounding" nature of Black loss.[4]

This book is animated by my deep interest in the Black ordinary as a space that contemporary Black feminist writing has largely jettisoned in the service of charting a different kind of ordinariness: the routinization of anti-Black violence. There is this, of course, and the ubiquity of regularized anti-Black violence must be documented. But there is also the arrangement of pins, to borrow from Christina Sharpe; there are also forsythia and zinnias; there is also the "ordinary note of care," which can—often *does*—take the form of paper towels purchased at Target, food poured into a Tupperware, a slow walk around the block. There are the forms of Black loss and Black living in the midst of loss that never take the form of state violence that, I think, we must also be able to offer an account of.

In this book I argue that beauty is central to how Black feminists write now, that it is the voice we have honed to write about our central preoccupation—loss. Beauty is not an antidote to loss. Indeed, as I have argued here, for Black feminists, beauty is a way of living with loss, a mode of writing and thinking loss, a practice of staying as close to loss as possible even as loss proves an elusive object, one where proximity and distance are often paired. If beauty is a method for staying close to loss, and for insisting that loss requires companionship, beautiful writing also reveals to us again and again that closeness is not always as clear as we might think it to be. This writing aspires to take us as close as it can to the scene of loss, only to find that the scene can be elusive. And this might be where beautiful writing is at its most powerful—when it sits with uncertainty and mystery, ambivalence and unknowing.

This book is motivated by a desire to think about what a dominant account of Black loss occludes or omits, and a wish to think about other forms of losing and loss that are indeed Black but cannot be seen as such in the framework that Black feminism advances. Where is the space for the ways that loss is often lived and felt in the parameters of the ordinary—where the ordinary is not merely a site of anti-Black violence but also a site of other forms of living, breathing, and doing? How might Black feminist theory hold space for ordinary losses and their quiet and still-urgent reverberations?

Ultimately, this book attempts to perform two kinds of work: to think about how we write now as entrenching a mode of thinking Black loss that can neglect the durational, the slow, the nonspectacular, and to think about how we can—and *must*—write now to unsettle that dominant account, to think about Black ordinariness as a rich archive for Black feminist thought. It is an insistence that to write (and read) for the Black ordinary is a refusal of the markets that have been set up to peddle in Black grief and that now tacitly require Black women to again and again speak our pain for an imagined national healing. I want to write now in a way that "stays at the bone," even as I want to refuse the markets and prying eyes that want to see Black pain and commodify it. I want to "stay at the bone," but I do not want Black pain to be what garners awards and prizes, tenures and promotions.[5] I want to "stay at the bone" not because I think we can access the truth of loss through beauty, but because I think that loss requires companionship and that this is a Black feminist ethic. I want to "stay at the bone" even when it is not always clear to me how we identify what constitutes the bone, or how deep the bone goes. I know that

I want to "stay at the bone" because I cannot write what matters to me—loss and its duration—without attending to its materiality.

But really, if I am honest with myself, what brought me to write this book was an interest in studying how Black feminists think about living with loss. This is because loss doesn't end and because loss is endless. It morphs and endures; it is reconfigured and transformed. For me, this book has been a departure from how I ordinarily write—perhaps, as my students might say, a writing that becomes possible after tenure when I have secured the requisite freedom to experiment. But there was no other way for me to write now, in the midst of my own sense of grief, in a moment where, thinking with Jesmyn Ward, I wear my loss like a "tender second skin."[6] The writing that I take up here is both my object of study and a tool that I have mobilized to live with my own pain. I have lived with Black feminist theory as I have lived with my mother's slow decline and my own sense of the ground constantly shifting beneath my feet.

Writing this book has helped me understand the dense desires that attend to the practice of writing for Black feminists—or at least for me. I have come to realize that I bring to this project an abiding wish for a bit more time, always just a bit more time, to be my mother's daughter.

NOTES

Preface

1   Endless thanks to Robyn Wiegman.

2   Williams, *Rooster's Egg*, 219.

3   Sharpe, *In the Wake*, 133.

4   Sharpe, *In the Wake*, 6.

5   My thinking here is shaped by Patricia J. Williams's insight. "So all of this leaves me feeling porous, unsettled, having lost the coherence of an identity I had thought of as my own. It brings felt meaning to the koan that novelist and Zen master Ruth Ozeki frequently cites as her meditative inspiration: 'What did your face look like before your parents were born?'" Williams, "Gathering the Ghosts."

6   I am channeling the opening pages of Williams's *The Alchemy of Race and Rights*. She writes, "You should know you are dealing with someone who is writing this in an old terry bathrobe with a little fringe of blue and white tassels dangling from the hem, trying to decide if she is stupid or crazy" (4).

7   My understanding of feminist stories is indebted to Clare Hemmings's *Why Stories Matter*.

8   Williams, "Gathering the Ghosts."

Chapter 1
Beauty, or, All about Black Feminist Theory's Mothers

1   As I write this, I am deeply grateful for Janelle Taylor's formulation. In "On Recognition," Taylor notes:

And I begin to see, too, that Mom has her own experience of the world that is different from mine, and interesting in its own way. The loosening of memory that leaves her stranded in the present moment also allows her to inhabit it more fully than I am able to, caught up as I always am in the rush of my days, so full of schedules, deadlines, plans and arrangements . . . Our conversations go nowhere, but it hardly matters what we say, really, or whether we said it before, or whether it is accurate or interesting or even comprehensible. The exchange itself is the point. (327)

I am also indebted to—and moved by—Taylor's notion that "she may not 'recognize' me in a narrowly cognitive sense, but my Mom does 'recognize' me as someone who is there with her, someone familiar perhaps, and she does not need to have all the details sorted out in order to 'care' for me" (329). Thanks to Sara Goering for bringing Taylor's work to my attention during my visit to the University of Washington.

2   Sharpe, *In the Wake*.

3   Elizabeth Alexander echoes this: "I am a Black mother of two Black sons. I exult in them, their accomplishments and happiness and struggles. And I worry about them so deeply it enters what sleep I have, from time to time, and I dream, when I am not exhausted, dream my worries for them. Every Black mother I know is exhausted in her own way." Alexander, *Trayvon Generation*, 119. In my earlier book, *Birthing Black Mothers*, I track how grief and loss have become synonyms for Black motherhood.

4   Alexander, "Trayvon Generation."

5   Tindal, "'Its Own Special Attraction,'" 259.

6   For key texts in an archive of theorizing Black loss, see Sharpe, *In the Wake*; McKittrick, "Mathematics Black Life"; K. Brown, "Black Elegies"; Evans, "Relentlessness of Black Grief"; Woubshet, *Calendar of Loss*; Abdur-Rahman, "Tenuous Hold"; Hartman, "Venus in Two Acts"; and Rankine, "Condition of Black Life." Rankine powerfully writes:

We live in a country where Americans assimilate corpses in their daily comings and goings. Dead blacks are a part of normal life here. Dying in ship hulls, tossed into the Atlantic, hanging from trees, beaten, shot in churches, gunned down by the police or warehoused in prisons: Historically, there is no quotidian without the enslaved, chained or dead black body to gaze upon or to hear about or to position a self against. When blacks become overwhelmed by our culture's disorder and protest (ultimately to our own detriment, because protest gives the police justification to militarize, as they did in Ferguson), the wrongheaded question that is asked is, What kind of savages are we? Rather than, What kind of country do we live in?

Also, Da'Shaun Harrison writes:

what i am seeking to clarify on our understanding of grief is that total healing is not possible for Black folks precisely because we exist as the underbelly of humanity and are therefore always grieving, as we live in Grief. if we accept that to be healed means to have grieved, as opposed to actively grieving, then there is no way for Black folks to ever be healed. i don't believe complete healing is possible for Black folks in an antiblack world; in a world wherein we are experiencing "the afterlife of slavery," as Saidiya Hartman names it. these thoughts force me to contend with the fact that grief, particularly for Black folks, is often a tension held in our bodies passed down from those who come before us; which is to say that grief is a communal process and practice that is rarely problematized beyond the individual. that's what i am seeking to do here: in Grief.

7   As I use the term *professional*, I am mindful of Tressie McMillan Cottom's insight in *Thick*:

Where black women have excelled is in the pursuit of legal authority, or the technical qualifications of social status. We go to school. We will, on average, go to all the school that the constraints on our time and money will allow us. . . . [B]lack women strive for forms of professional status. We start businesses at surprisingly high rates given how little family wealth we have to draw on or social networks we have to support us. We perform phenomenally high rates of community service and lay leadership in churches, schools, and civic organizations. We are, it could be argued, professional professionals. (20–21)

I also write this mindful of Darlene Clark Hine's historically grounded insights on Black women's practices of "dissemblance." See Hine, "Rape."

8   Quashie, *Sovereignty of Quiet*, 6.

9   My understanding of the ordinary is indebted to Kathleen Stewart's work in *Ordinary Affects*. Stewart notes, "The ordinary is a shifting assemblage of practices and practical knowledges, a scene of both liveness and exhaustion, a dream of escape or of the simple life. Ordinary affects are the varied, surging capacities to affect and to be affected that give everyday life the quality of a continual motion of relations, scenes, contingencies, and emergences. They're things that happen" (1–2).

10   See Freeman, *Time Binds*. I am also indebted to work on "crip time." Ellen Samuels notes, "*Crip time is time travel.* Disability and illness have the power to extract us from linear, progressive time with its normative life stages and cast us into a wormhole of backward and forward acceleration, jerky stops and starts, tedious intervals and abrupt endings." Samuels, "Six Ways of Looking."

11   Morgan, *When Chickenheads Come Home*, 83. I am drawing on Patricia Hill Collins's foundational work on controlling images in *Black Feminist Thought*.

12   Eng and Kazanjian, "Mourning Remains," 1.

13   Eng and Kazanjian, "Mourning Remains," 1.

14   I take this up more in my earlier article "Writing Black Beauty." Here I return to Patricia Williams's work, which—in her plea to restore the place of rights in critical legal projects—argues that we need to "give to all of society's objects and untouchables the rights of privacy, integrity, and self-assertion; give them distance and respect." Williams, *Alchemy*, 165. I also think with Christina Sharpe, who writes, "My mother was a very private person. I do not know whether her privacy was by choice or circumstance. I do know that what I learn in this exchange is just some small part of my mother's life. Those other parts of her life about which I know next to nothing: I have tried to enter with grace and imagine with tenderness or I have left them alone. I owe my mother that. Regard." Sharpe, *Ordinary Notes*, 232.

15   I am thinking with Kevin Quashie's provocation "What if black feminism is supposed to teach us how to feel?" posed at Duke's Black Feminist Theory Summer Institute in 2022. I am grateful for his presence there.

16   Williams, *Alchemy*, 19.

17   There are many ways this sentiment gets articulated: Barbara Christian famously wrote, "I can only speak for myself. But what I write and how I write is done in order to save my life. And I mean that literally." Christian, "Race for Theory," 61. Writing by scholars in public forms—like Sami Schalk's Twitter—insists, "Black feminism changed my life. Black feminists saved my life. I will always be a black feminist." Schalk, Twitter, March 22, 2019, 8:41 a.m., https://twitter.com/DrSamiSchalk/status/1109087710042640391.

18   Sharpe, *In the Wake*, 10; Williams, "Gathering the Ghosts"; and José Esteban Muñoz, quoted in Chambers-Letson, *After the Party*, xvii.

19 My understanding of being moved is indebted to both Deborah Gould's *Moving Politics* and Jennifer Doyle's *Hold It against Me*.

20 Williams, *Alchemy*, 92.

21 Hartman, *Scenes of Subjection*, 88.

22 Sharpe, "Beauty Is a Method."

23 Hartman, *Wayward Lives*, 33. I am reminded of how Alice Walker describes her mother as "the woman who literally covered the holes in our walls with sunflowers." Walker, *Search*, 242.

24 Sharpe, "Beauty Is a Method."

25 Sharpe, "Beauty Is a Method."

26 Alexander, "Trayvon Generation."

27 Alexander, "Trayvon Generation."

28 Alexander is not alone in representing Black dancing bodies as an image of freedom. At the end of "Selling Hot Pussy," bell hooks offers an analysis of films that she argues subvert the dominant gaze, including Sankofa's *Passion of Remembrance*, where two young Black women get dressed to go out for the evening and begin dancing together.

29 Alexander, "Trayvon Generation."

30 Alexander, "Trayvon Generation."

31 See Nash, *Birthing Black Mothers*.

32 Williams, *Alchemy*, 217.

33 Articulated another way, this is the search for "her shape and his hand," as Williams notes. Williams, *Alchemy,* 19.

34 Bey, *Black Trans Feminism*, 33.

35 Walker, *Search*, 243.

36 Sharpe, *Ordinary Notes*, 351, 26. Laura Briggs takes up the risks of speaking of mothers in her recent work, noting that she is "struggling with words like 'women' and 'mothers' in this book." Briggs, *How All Politics*, 5.

37 Sharpe, "Beauty Is a Method."

38 Sharpe, "Beauty Is a Method."

39 Sharpe's *Ordinary Notes*, published just as I was finishing this manuscript, evidences another method of Black beautiful writing: the note.

40 Sharpe, "Beauty Is a Method."

41 Sharpe, "Beauty Is a Method."

42 I am borrowing from Elizabeth Spires's poem "Globe": "Memory's false as anything, spliced in the wrong parts, / queerly jumping. But better than forgetting." Spires, "Globe."

43 Behar, *Vulnerable Observer*, 13.

44 I take this up in more detail in my review of *Wayward Lives*. See Nash, review.

45 Hartman, *Wayward Lives*, xiv.

46 Hartman, *Wayward Lives*, xiv.

47 Hartman, *Wayward Lives*, 60.

48 Sharpe, "Beauty Is a Method."

49 Sharpe, "Beauty Is a Method."

50 Sharpe, *Ordinary Notes*, 17.

51 Scarry, *On Beauty*, 2.

52 Sharpe, "Beauty Is a Method."

53 As I note elsewhere, afropessimist work has traveled citationally with Black feminist scholars including Hortense Spillers, Saidiya Hartman, Christina Sharpe, and Katherine McKittrick. See Nash, "On the Beginning."

54 Wilderson, *Afropessimism*, 15. Wilderson's investment in the erotic and sadomasochistic dimensions of race is in dialogue with Anthony Paul Farley's body of work, particularly "The Black Body as Fetish Object."

55 Rich, "Notes" 224.

56 Rich, "Notes," 225.

57 Wiegman, *Object Lessons*, 13.

58 For more on a critique of how contemporary feminism figures "white women" and "white feminism," see Nash and Pinto, "New Genealogy."

59 See Chowdhury and Philipose, *Dissident Friendships*. Chambers-Letson, *After the Party*, 9.

60 Chambers-Letson, *After the Party*, xii.

61 Bay et al., "Toward an Intellectual History," 2.

62 See Christian, "Race for Theory."

63 Christian, "Race for Theory"; Hill Collins, "Learning from the Outsider Within"; Williams, *Alchemy*. Christian also recognized the centrality of pleasure, play, and "grace" to Black women's theorizing: "And women, at least the women I grew up around, continuously speculated about

the nature of life through pithy language that unmasked the power relations of their world. It is this language, and the grace and pleasure with which they played with it, that I find celebrated, refined, critiqued in the works of writers like Toni Morrison and Alice Walker. My folk, in other words, have always been a race for theory—though more in the form of the hieroglyph, a written figure that is both sensual and abstract, both beautiful and communicative." Christian, "Race for Theory," 52.

64   As examples of the visibility of this work, I am thinking about the new proliferation of Black feminist academics writing trade books, perhaps most visible in Christina Sharpe's *Ordinary Notes*, and the visibility of this work, including the *New York Times*' profile of Sharpe, describing her as "the woman shaping a generation of black thought" and the *New Yorker*'s profile of Hartman. See Wortham, "Woman Shaping a Generation"; and Okeowo, "How Saidiya Hartman Retells." Jenna Wortham writes, "Sharpe is part of a cohort of thinkers and artists—including Hartman, Arthur Jafa, Fred Moten, Simone Leigh, Garrett Bradley, Ja'Tovia Gary, Lorraine O'Grady and others—who are interrogating the rendering of Blackness in American culture and offering new ways of looking, seeing and being seen."

65   Moraga and Anzaldúa, *This Bridge Called My Back*, 21.

66   Moraga and Anzaldúa, *This Bridge Called My Back*, 21.

67   I am thinking of Brittney Cooper, Keeanga-Yamahtta Taylor, Salamishah Tillet, Imani Perry, Ange-Marie Hancock, Melissa Harris-Perry, and Treva Lindsey, among others. For popular coverage of *Wayward Lives*, see Okeowo, "How Saidiya Hartman Retells"; Sehgal, "Exhilarating Work of History"; and Gordon-Reed, "Rebellious History." For popular coverage of *In the Wake*, see Parul Sehgal noting, "My most valuable discovery was the work of Christina Sharpe, a scholar of breathtaking range whose most recent book is *In the Wake* about the aftershocks of chattel slavery in the Americas." Sehgal, in Garner, Sehgal, and Szalai, "Times Critics Discuss." Simone Leigh notes, "So many contemporary artists and scholars have been changed by the book 'In the Wake: On Blackness and Being,' by Christina Sharpe, which examines the legacy of black death in the context of chattel slavery." Leigh, in Leigh, Sherald, and Simpson, "'I Want to Explore.'"

68   See duCille, "Occult of True Black Womanhood."

69   Alexander, "Trayvon Generation."

70   Alexander, "Trayvon Generation."

71 Harris, "People Are Marching."

72 Harris, "Books on Race."

73 Jackson, "What Is an Anti-racist Reading List For?"

74 Brittney Cooper eloquently makes this point in *Beyond Respectability*.

75 Williams, *Alchemy*, 7.

76 Alexander, "Trayvon Generation."

77 Hong, "'Future of Our Worlds,'" 96.

78 Hong, "'Future of Our Worlds,'" 96.

Chapter 2
Staying at the Bone

Epigraph: Elizabeth Alexander, in Galanes, "Sheryl Sandberg and Elizabeth Alexander," https://www.nytimes.com/2017/05/13/fashion/sheryl-sandberg-and-elizabeth-alexander-on-love-loss-and-what-comes-next.html.

1 Galanes, "Sheryl Sandberg and Elizabeth Alexander."

2 Alexander, *Light of the World*, 1.

3 Alexander, in Galanes, "Sheryl Sandberg and Elizabeth Alexander." This notion of writing as "placing my hand on the earth," and of writing loss as a "steady companion," is echoed by other Black feminists who describe writing loss as a form of living with it, and a practice of staying close to those who have died. Edwidge Danticat notes, "Writing has been the primary way I have tried to make sense of my losses, including deaths. I have been writing about death for as long as I have been writing. . . . Now that my father and mother and many other people I love have died I want to both better understand death and offload my fear of it, and I believe reading and writing can help." Danticat, *Art of Death*, 6.

4 Rich, "Notes," 181.

5 Friedman, "Respair."

6 Ward, "Witness and Respair."

7 Ward, "Witness and Respair."

8 Ward, "Witness and Respair."

9 Ward, "Witness and Respair."

10 Ward, "Witness and Respair."

11 Ward, "Witness and Respair."

12 Lewis, "Where Are the Photos."

13 "An Incalculable Loss," *New York Times.*

14 Melanye Price writes, "I don't know if it's ethical, though, to repeatedly show and share what are essentially snuff films with African-American protagonists. The news media must rethink their decisions to binge broadcast these images and reconsider how much of the content should be shown." Price, "Please Stop Showing the Video."

   Also, Wesley Morris notes, "The most urgent filmmaking anybody's doing in this country right now is by black people with camera phones. Their work comprises a ghastly visual mosaic of mistreatment, at best, and whose victims are international symbols of mourning: Eric Garner, Philando Castile, Sandra Bland. Art is not the intent. These videos are the stone truth. Quaking proof of insult, seasick funerals. Livestreamed or uploaded, or suppressed then suspiciously unearthed as found footage." Morris, "Videos That Rocked America."

15 Alexander, in Tillet, "Endless Grief."

16 Ward, "Witness and Respair."

17 Gordinier, "Elizabeth Alexander."

18 Alexander, *Light of the World,* 9.

19 Griffin, quoted in Gordinier, "Elizabeth Alexander."

20 Alexander, *Light of the World,* 169.

21 Alexander, *Light of the World,* 76.

22 Alexander, *Light of the World,* 47.

23 Alexander, *Light of the World,* 49.

24 Alexander, *Light of the World,* 50.

25 Alexander, *Light of the World,* 43.

26 Alexander, *Light of the World,* 101.

27 Alexander, *Light of the World,* 38.

28 See Geronimus, *Weathering.*

29 Alexander, *Light of the World,* 33.

30 Alexander, quoted in Gordinier, "Elizabeth Alexander."

31 Alexander, *Light of the World,* 110.

32 Alexander, *Light of the World,* 98.

33 Alexander, *Light of the World,* 203.

34 Trethewey, *Memorial Drive,* 189.

35 Trethewey, *Memorial Drive*, 205.

36 Trethewey, *Memorial Drive*, 6.

37 Trethewey, *Memorial Drive*, 6.

38 Trethewey, *Memorial Drive*, 7.

39 Trethewey, *Memorial Drive*, 199.

40 Trethewey, *Memorial Drive*, 178.

41 Trethewey, *Memorial Drive*, 178.

42 Trethewey, *Memorial Drive*, 51.

43 Trethewey, *Memorial Drive*, 204.

44 Trethewey, *Memorial Drive*, 213.

45 Adichie, *Notes on Grief*, 24.

46 Alexander, *Light of the World*, 177.

47 Spires, "Globe."

Chapter 3
An Invitation to Listen

1   Brelis, "You've Got Male!"

2   Perry, *Breathe*, 15.

3   Fulton, "If They Refuse."

4   Wines and Goode, "Cities Rocked by Past Protests."

5   Fulton, "If They Refuse."

6   Fulton, "If They Refuse."

7   Purnell, "Grief over Time." Fulton says, "Before I lost Trayvon, I can tell you I was living just a regular life. I had not been to a march at all. I'm not telling people, you know, that 'Oh, I've been this community activist all my life.' No, I have not."

8   Fulton, "If They Refuse."

9   Emily Owens analyzes Fulton's letter as one where "Fulton asks us to slow down enough to feel. . . . She asks us to feel, to mourn, and to yearn for a world in which black and brown children get to grow up." My work here is indebted to her analysis in "'We Have to Make Them Feel Us.'"

10 Hamilton, review; and Lordi, "Between the World and the Addressee," 436.

11 Owens, "'We Have to Make Them Feel Us.'"

12   Ratcliffe, "Eavesdropping as Rhetorical Tactic," 90.

13   See Lugones, "Playfulness."

14   See Gordon, *Ghostly Matters*.

15   Lordi, "Between the World and the Addressee," 435.

16   Coates, *Between the World and Me*, 9.

17   Coates, *Between the World and Me*, 103.

18   Coates, *Between the World and Me*, 12.

19   Bennett, "Ta-Nehisi Coates."

20   M. Alexander, "Ta-Nehisi Coates's 'Between the World and Me.'"

21   Hamilton, review.

22   In "What Is an Anti-Racist Reading List For?" Lauren Michele Jackson writes:

> Despite the diversity of curators—from legacy publications to small non-profits to historians to celebrities and other users with varying degrees of influence online (to your next door neighbor, probably)—the anti-racist reading list varies little in its contents. The usual subjects are as long as the list themselves, we could chant them together: *Sister Outsider*, *The Fire Next Time*, *Between the World and Me*, *The Autobiography of Malcolm X*, *The New Jim Crow*, *Their Eyes Were Watching God*, *Women, Race, & Class*; maybe *The Wretched of the Earth* or *Black Skin, White Masks* if someone took a postcolonial theory course in college. With the exception of Ta-Nehisi Coates or Michelle Alexander or Claudia Rankine, contemporary titles on the list tend to baldly demonstrate the rise in general reader interest in how-to, come-to-Jesus talks about race. Race readers, I like to call them, books like Ijeoma Oluo's *So You Want to Talk About Race*, Crystal Marie Fleming's *How to Be Less Stupid About Race*, and the mac daddies of the bunch, *How to Be an Antiracist* by Ibram X. Kendi and *White Fragility* by Robin DiAngelo.

23   Brit Bennett thinks about this question in her review ("Ta-Nehisi Coates and a Generation Waking Up"), noting:

> Although the book has been widely praised as a monumental text about black life, it's more specifically a book about how to live free in a black male body. . . . Coates describes black women lovingly, almost ethereally, but they rarely appear as complicated, fully fleshed-out people. He closes the book with a conversation with Mabel Jones, his dead classmate's mother. Her loss, to Coates, is

her "legacy," the time and energy and love she poured into a son who was stolen from her. Jones worries about her daughter—not about her daughter's own body but about her daughter birthing a son whose body she could not protect from "the ritual violence that had claimed" her own brother. Here, black women are vulnerable because of their love for black men. Coates writes extensively about the vulnerability of the black body, but he only briefly alludes to the additional ways black women's bodies are vulnerable to sexual and physical violence. To his credit, he does not presume to be an expert on black women's experiences, but his reluctance to interrogate them further feels odd for a narrator who is otherwise insatiably curious. "The women around you must be responsible for their bodies in a way that you never will know," he writes to his son, and the lesson stops there. The dangers of living in a black female body are mysterious, forever unknowable.

24 Young, "Black Mother Reflects."

25 Nicole Fleetwood has also contributed an important essay to this archive. See Fleetwood, "Raising a Black Boy."

26 See, for example, Morris, "Black women write love letters." While it remains the case that these letters take a particular interest in Black sons, in the wake of Breonna Taylor's murder in 2020, there was a new attention to the violence that Black girls face. In 2021 the *New York Times* asked Black mothers to write open letters to their daughters. In one letter, a mother writes:

> Let go of what the media portrays about the value of your life. Let go of the idea that your color determines anything about you. Let go of the idea that your gender determines anything for you. Let go of the guilt and shame that too often come with being a woman who does, feels and expresses as she pleases. Let go of systems that try to put you in a checkbox. You're bigger than that. You are stronger than that. You are wiser than that. You are smarter than that. There is nothing too broad, or anything too deep that you cannot possess. You are the curator of your reality. (Peck, "To My Daughter.")

27 Griffin, "Radical Love Letter."

28 Griffin, "Radical Love Letter."

29 Griffin, "Radical Love Letter."

30 Sewing, "Letter to My Black Son."

31 Sewing, "Letter to My Black Son."

32   Sewing, "Letter to My Black Son."

33   Perry, *Breathe*, 9.

34   Alexander, "Trayvon Generation." Perry, *Breathe*, 17.

35   Perry, *Breathe*, 66.

36   Chambers-Letson, *After the Party*, 4.

37   Perry, *Breathe*, 21.

38   Perry, *Breathe*, 149.

39   Perry, *Breathe*, 150.

40   Perry, *Breathe*, 150.

41   Perry, *Breathe*, 157.

42   Perry, "Stop Hustling Black Death."

43   *Community property* is Karla Holloway's term. Holloway, *Passed On*, 8.

44   Rice quoted in Smith, "Samaria Rice rebukes Tamika Mallory."

45   See Woubshet, *Calendar of Loss*.

46   Singh, *Breaks*, 21.

47   Singh, *Breaks*, 9.

48   Singh, *Breaks*, 11.

49   I find myself thinking of Breonna Taylor gunned down in her home, or Korryn Gaines gunned down in her own car. And I find myself thinking of earlier cases of Black women murdered in their homes, like Eleanor Bumpurs. My thinking here is indebted, also, to hearing Sarah Haley present her work on the violence inflicted on Black women's homes by police. See, for example, Haley, "Radical Potential."

50   Singh, *Breaks*, 22.

51   Singh, *Breaks*, 23.

52   Singh, *Breaks*, 141.

53   Singh, *Breaks*, 141.

54   I think of those lines from Philip Levine's beautiful poem "Facts," in *What Work Is*, 24.

> I feel the bulk of me shrinking, becoming
> more frail and delicate. I get cold easily as though

I lacked even the solidity to protect my own heart.

55   I am reminded of Marie Howe's "What the Living Do," in *What the Living Do*, 89:

Johnny, the kitchen sink has been clogged for days, some utensil
probably fell down there.

And the Drano won't work but smells dangerous, and the crusty
dishes have piled up waiting for the plumber I still haven't called. This
is the everyday we spoke of. . . . [I]t's winter again: the sky's a deep,
headstrong blue, and the sunlight pours through the open living-room
windows because the heat's on too high in here and I can't turn it off.

For weeks now, driving, or dropping a bag of groceries in the
street, the bag breaking, I've been thinking: This is what the living do.

Chapter 4
Picturing Loss

Epigraph: Patricia J. Williams, "Gathering the Ghosts," https://
alinejournal.com/vol-1-no-3-4/gathering-the-ghosts/.

1   Sharpe, *In the Wake*, 23. This is a project Sharpe takes up in more detail in
     Ordinary Notes, asking, "What would a camera lucida of the Black ma-
     ternal look like? What would it trace?" (167). In a later note, she writes,
     "These particular photographs are of my mother's face, her hands, her
     books, her needlework; my camera lucida is saturated with my seeing
     and my mother's care in the noise of structural precarity" (169).

2   Sharpe, *In the Wake*, 13, 10. Sharpe writes, "I've been trying to articu-
     late a method of encountering a past that is not past. A method along
     the lines of sitting with, a gathering, and a tracking of phenomena that
     disproportionately and devastatingly affect Black peoples any and ev-
     erywhere we are. I've been thinking of this gathering, this collecting
     and reading toward a new analytic, as the wake, and wake work" (13).

3   Sharpe, *In the Wake*, 19. In "Minor Revolutionaries," Jack Halberstam
     makes a similar claim about the new grammars that Saidiya Hartman's
     Wayward Lives, Beautiful Experiments develops. Halberstam writes:

     The lexicon of the wayward includes: exorbitant, intimate, assem-
     bly, terrible, symphony, chorus, sensation, experiment, social poesis,
     fugitive gestures, unregulated movement, not to mention leaderless
     swarm, rambling, cruising, smashing, unrepentant, ungovernable
     wants, open rebellion, terrible beauty, black music, and so on. These
     are not the words we usually find in either history or literary analy-
     sis, and this vocabulary signals a break with the dry work of telling,
     explaining, proving, proposing, illustrating, clarifying, identify-

ing, naming, showing. The vocabulary that Hartman favors is that of excess and extravagance. In using these terms, she leads us away from the labors of academia and its grim insistence on knowing and understanding and offers an entryway into an energetic world of gesture, struggle, collaboration, and improvised life.

4 Sharpe, *In the Wake*, 13.

5 Williams, "Gathering the Ghosts."

6 Williams, "Gathering the Ghosts."

7 There is a robust body of feminist scholarship on the family photograph, including Campt, *Listening to Images*; Hirsch, *Family Frames*; Kuhn, *Family Secrets*; Phu and Brown, "Cultural Politics of Aspiration"; and E. Brown and Davidmann, "Queering the Trans Family Album."

8 I am thinking with Jennifer Morgan's analysis of Hortense Spillers's work on "kinfulness" at the Duke Feminist Theory Workshop 2022.

9 There are many fantasies about the past that animate contemporary Black feminist thought, particularly its public life, in refrains like "I am my ancestors' wildest dreams."

10 Campt, *Listening to Images*.

11 Here, I think of Toni Morrison's dedication to *Sula*:

> It is sheer good fortune to miss
> somebody long before they leave you.
> This book is for Ford and Slade, whom
> I miss although they have not left me. (xi)

12 Fleetwood, "Posing in Prison," 488.

13 Fleetwood, "Posing in Prison," 499.

14 Fleetwood, "Posing in Prison," 488.

15 Fleetwood, "Posing in Prison," 488.

16 Fleetwood, "Posing in Prison," 488.

17 Campt, *Image Matters*, 201.

18 Campt, *Image Matters*, 202.

19 Campt, *Image Matters*, 202.

20 Campt, *Image Matters*, 202.

21 At the end of Williams's *The Alchemy of Race and Rights*, she offers a "Word on Categories" describing her editor's "struggle" with the Library of Congress about how to classify her book: "The librarians think 'Afro-Americans—Civil Rights' and 'Law Teachers' would be nice. I told

my editor to hold out for 'Autobiography,' 'Fiction,' 'Gender Studies,' and 'Medieval Medicine'" (256–57).

22 Quoted in Okeowo, "How Saidiya Hartman Retells."

23 Quoted in Okeowo, "How Saidiya Hartman Retells." Kevin Quashie describes *Wayward Lives* as a "historical novel" and notes that it is "a book of anecdotal choreographed scenes of the ordinary." Quashie, "Flash of Light," 124.

24 Hartman, quoted in Okeowo, "How Saidiya Hartman Retells."

25 Okeowo, "How Saidiya Hartman Retells."

26 Hartman, *Wayward Lives*, xiii.

27 Hartman narrates her own experience of completing *Wayward Lives* as shaped by loss. She describes how she had completed the manuscript and then lost her mother. As she says, "The footnotes were incomplete. In this grief-filled state, it was hard to imagine completing this gargantuan task." Hartman, "Intimate History, Radical Narrative," 127.

28 Hartman, "Venus in Two Acts," 4.

29 Hartman, *Wayward Lives*, xv.

30 Hartman describes "intimate history" as an "effort to convey the revolution of Black intimate life in the twentieth century and it names the style of close narration that is utilized in the book. It reckons with the violence of history by 'crafting a love letter to all those who had been harmed.'" Hartman, "Intimate History, Radical Narrative," 129.

31 Hartman, "Intimate History, Radical Narrative," 135.

32 Hartman, *Wayward Lives*, 20.

33 Morgan, Duke Feminist Theory Workshop, Spring 2022.

34 See Nash, "*Wayward Lives* Review."

35 Hartman, *Wayward Lives*, 33.

36 Hartman, *Wayward Lives*, 33.

37 Sharpe, "Beauty Is a Method." Elaine Scarry advances a similar argument, noting, "When the eye sees something beautiful the hand wants to draw it." Scarry, *On Beauty*, 1.

38 Hartman, *Wayward Lives*, xx.

39 Hartman, *Wayward Lives*, xiv.

40 Hartman, *Wayward Lives*, xv.

41 Williams, "Gathering the Ghosts."

42   Quashie echoes these queries about an image of a young Black girl on a sofa titled "A Minor Figure" in Hartman's book. Quashie asks, "Is it that the world of the book could sustain this and other tender moments, that the whole of it is a cushion of regard so that the visual and narrative apparatuses would not conjure only the pornographic?" Quashie, "A Flash of Life and Light," 125.

43   Hartman, *Wayward Lives*, 298.

44   Hartman, *Wayward Lives*, 314.

45   Hartman, *Wayward Lives*, 347.

46   Hartman, *Wayward Lives*, 348.

47   Hartman, *Wayward Lives*, 349.

48   In her analysis of "black femme praxis," Treva Ellison develops the term *flocking*—alongside adrienne maree brown's work—to describe the "aesthetic and gestural adaptations" that Black femmes make "in order to move through space and survive." She writes, "Flocking creates the possibility for Black trans and queer aesthetics through collective practice rather than carceral capture and coercion." Ellison, "Black Femme Praxis," 13.

49   Hartman, *Wayward Lives*, 348.

50   Williams, "Gathering the Ghosts."

51   Williams, "Gathering the Ghosts."

52   Williams, On Being the "Object of Property."

53   Williams, "Gathering the Ghosts."

54   I am reminded of Tina Campt's note: "The idea of photography as only a record of past experiences is something I fundamentally disagree with. If we think about it grammatically, photography is always about positioning yourself in a way that projects you into the future—not necessarily a future that will happen, but the future that you want to happen, the way you want to be perceived in the future. And that future is not decades in the future, it is right now, today, right after the shot is taken." Campt, "Sound of Defiance."

55   Williams, *Alchemy*, 155.

56   Williams, *Alchemy*, 19. For more on "her shape and his hand," see Avery Gordon's engagement with it in *Ghostly Matters*.

57   Williams, "Gathering the Ghosts."

58   Williams, "Gathering the Ghosts."

59   Williams, "Gathering the Ghosts."

60   Williams, "Gathering the Ghosts."

61   Williams, *Alchemy*, 217.

Conclusion
New Furniture, or, All about Black Feminist Theory's Fathers

Epigraph: Muñoz, "Vitalism's After-Burn,"191.

1   Sharpe, *In the Wake*, 133.

2   Berlant and Warner, "What Does Queer Theory Teach Us," 345.

3   Samantha Pinto and I wrote about Black maternal memoirs, including Sybrina Fulton and Tracy Martin's co-written memoir, *Rest in Power*, about their son Trayvon Martin's murder. We gesture to the fact that the memoir is largely Fulton's story. One cannot help but wonder about the markets that make her grief commodifiable and about where Martin's grief goes, what cultural space exists for it. See Nash and Pinto, "Strange Intimacies."

4   See Woubshet, *Calendar of Loss*, 4.

5   As Emily Owens said about her own memoir-inspired work presented at the Black Feminist Theory Summer Institute in 2022, "I do not want this book to be useful." Emily Owens, Duke University, "Body Story," August 2022.

6   Ward, "Witness and Respair."

BIBLIOGRAPHY

Abdur-Rahman, Aliyyah I. "A Tenuous Hold." *Black Scholar* 49, no. 2 (2019): 38–43.

Abrams, Stacey. *Our Time Is Now: Power, Purpose, and the Fight for a Fair America*. New York: Henry Holt, 2020.

Adichie, Chimamanda Ngozi. *Notes on Grief*. New York: Knopf, 2021.

Alexander, Elizabeth. *The Light of the World: A Memoir*. New York: Grand Central, 2015.

Alexander, Elizabeth. "The Trayvon Generation." *New Yorker*, June 22, 2020. https://www.newyorker.com/magazine/2020/06/22/the-trayvon -generation.

Alexander, Elizabeth. *The Trayvon Generation*. New York: Grand Central, 2022.

Alexander, Michelle. "Ta-Nehisi Coates's 'Between the World and Me.'" *New York Times*, August 17, 2015. https://www.nytimes.com/2015/08/17/books /review/ta-nehisi-coates-between-the-world-and-me.html.

Baldwin, James. *The Fire Next Time*. New York: Modern Library, 1995.

Bay, Mia, Farah J. Griffin, Martha S. Jones, and Barbara Savage. "Toward an Intellectual History of Black Women." In *Toward an Intellectual History of Black Women*, edited by Mia Bay, Farah J. Griffin, Martha S. Jones, and Barbara Savage, 1–15. Chapel Hill: University of North Carolina Press, 2015.

Behar, Ruth. *The Vulnerable Observer: Anthropology That Breaks Your Heart*. Boston: Beacon, 1996.

Bennett, Brit. "Ta-Nehisi Coates and a Generation Waking Up." *New Yorker*, July 15, 2015. https://www.newyorker.com/culture/cultural-comment/ta -nehisi-coates-and-a-generation-waking-up.

Berlant, Lauren, and Michael Warner. "What Does Queer Theory Teach Us about X?" *PMLA* 110, no. 3 (1995): 343–49.

Bey, Marquis. *Black Trans Feminism*. Durham, NC: Duke University Press, 2022.

Brelis, Matthew. "You've Got Male!" *Vassar Magazine*, January 2011. https://www.vassar.edu/vq/issues/2011/01/features/youve-got-male.html.

Briggs, Laura. *How All Politics Became Reproductive Politics: From Welfare Reform to Foreclosure to Trump*. Oakland: University of California Press, 2018.

Brown, Elspeth, and Sara Davidmann. "'Queering the Trans* Family Album': Elspeth H. Brown and Sara Davidmann, in Conversation." *Radical History Review* no. 122 (2015): 188–200.

Brown, Kimberly Juanita. "Black Elegies in Sight and Sound: Care Syllabus." Care Syllabus. https://www.caresyllabus.org/black-elegies-in-sight-and-sound. Accessed September 27, 2023.

Campt, Tina. *Image Matters: Archive, Photography, and the African Diaspora in Europe*. Durham, NC: Duke University Press, 2012.

Campt, Tina. *Listening to Images*. Durham, NC: Duke University Press, 2017.

Campt, Tina. "The Sound of Defiance." Interview by Brian Wallis. *Aperture*, October 15, 2017. https://aperture.org/editorial/tina-campt-conversation-brian-wallis/.

Chambers-Letson, Joshua. *After the Party: A Manifesto for Queer of Color Life*. New York: New York University Press, 2018.

Chowdhury, Elora, and Liz Philipose, eds. *Dissident Friendships: Feminism, Imperialism, and Transnational Solidarity*. Urbana: University of Illinois Press, 2016.

Christian, Barbara. "The Race for Theory." *Cultural Critique* 6 (1987): 51–63.

Coates, Ta-Nehisi. *Between the World and Me*. New York: Random House, 2015.

Cooper, Brittney C. *Beyond Respectability: The Intellectual Thought of Race Women*. Urbana: University of Illinois Press, 2017.

Cottom, Tressie McMillan. *Thick*. New York: New Press, 2019.

Danticat, Edwidge. *The Art of Death: Writing the Final Story*. Minneapolis: Graywolf, 2017.

Doyle, Jennifer. *Hold It against Me: Difficulty and Emotion in Contemporary Art*. Durham, NC: Duke University Press, 2013.

duCille, Ann. "The Occult of True Black Womanhood: Critical Demeanor and Black Feminist Studies." *Signs: A Journal of Women in Culture and Society* 19, no. 3 (1994): 591–629.

Ellison, Treva. "Black Femme Praxis and the Promise of Black Gender." *Black Scholar* 49, no. 1 (2019): 6–16.

Eng, David, and David Kazanjian. "Mourning Remains." In *Loss: The Politics of Mourning*, edited by David Eng and David Kazanjian. Berkeley: University of California Press, 2002: 1–28.

Evans, Marissa. "The Relentlessness of Black Grief." *Atlantic*, September 27, 2020. https://www.theatlantic.com/ideas/archive/2020/09/relentlessness-black-grief/616511/.

Farley, Anthony Paul. "The Black Body as Fetish Object." *Oregon Law Review* 76, no. 3 (1997): 457–535.

Fleetwood, Nicole R. *Marking Time: Art in the Age of Mass Incarceration*. Cambridge, MA: Harvard University Press, 2020.

Fleetwood, Nicole R. "Posing in Prison: Family Photographs, Emotional Labor, and Carceral Intimacy." *Public Culture* 27, no. 3 (2015): 487–511.

Fleetwood, Nicole R. "Raising a Black Boy Not to Be Afraid." Literary Hub, October 3, 2018. https://lithub.com/raising-a-black-boy-not-to-be-afraid/.

Freeman, Elizabeth. *Time Binds: Queer Temporalities, Queer Histories*. Durham, NC: Duke University Press, 2010.

Friedman, Nancy. "Respair." *Fritinancy* (blog), December 21, 2020. https://nancyfriedman.typepad.com/away_with_words/2020/12/word-of-the-week-respair.html.

Fulton, Sybrina. "If They Refuse to Hear Us, We Will Make Them Feel Us." *TIME* magazine, August 18, 2014. https://time.com/3136685/travyon-sybrina-fulton-ferguson/.

Fulton, Sybrina, and Tracy Martin. *Rest in Power: The Enduring Life of Trayvon Martin*. New York: Spiegel and Grau, 2017.

Galanes, Philip. "Sheryl Sandberg and Elizabeth Alexander on Love, Loss and What Comes Next." *New York Times*, May 13, 2017. https://www.nytimes.com/2017/05/13/fashion/sheryl-sandberg-and-elizabeth-alexander-on-love-loss-and-what-comes-next.html.

Garner, Dwight, Parul Sehgal, and Jennifer Szalai. "Times Critics Discuss the Year in Books, from Triumphs to Disappointments." *New York Times*, December 4, 2018. https://www.nytimes.com/2018/12/04/books/times-critics-discuss-the-year-in-books-from-triumphs-to-disappointments.html.

Geronimus, Arline. *Weathering: The Extraordinary Stress of Ordinary Life in an Unjust Society*. New York: Little, Brown Spark, 2023.

Gordinier, Jeff. "Elizabeth Alexander: Eat, Memory." *New York Times Style Magazine*, March 20, 2015. https://www.nytimes.com/2015/03/20/t-magazine/elizabeth-alexander-memoir-eat-memory.html.

Gordon, Avery. *Ghostly Matters: Haunting and the Sociological Imagination*. Minneapolis: University of Minnesota Press, 1997.

Gordon-Reed, Annette. "Rebellious History." *New York Review*, October 22, 2020. https://www.nybooks.com/articles/2020/10/22/saidiya-hartman-rebellious-history/.

Gould, Deborah. *Moving Politics: Emotion and ACT UP's Fight against AIDS*. Chicago: University of Chicago Press, 2009.

Griffin, Sarah Mantilla. "A Radical Love Letter to My Son." Feminist Wire, September 3, 2013. https://thefeministwire.com/2013/09/a-radical-love-letter-to-my-son/.

Gumbs, Alexis Pauline, China Martins, and Mai'a Williams, eds. *Revolutionary Mothering: Love on the Front Lines*. Oakland: PM Press, 2016.

Halberstam, Jack. "Minor Revolutionaries: A New Chapter in Queer Studies." *LA Review of Books*, July 21, 2019. https://lareviewofbooks.org/article/minor-revolutionaries-a-new-chapter-in-queer-studies/.

Haley, Sarah. "The Radical Potential of Black Feminist Evaluation." *GLQ: A Journal of Lesbian and Gay Studies* 25, no. 1 (2019): 178–82.

Hamilton, Jack. Review of *Between the World and Me*. *Slate*, July 9, 2015. https://slate.com/culture/2015/07/between-the-world-and-me-by-ta-nehisi-coates-reviewed.html.

Harris, Elizabeth A. "Books on Race Filled Best-Seller Lists Last Year. Publishers Took Notice." *New York Times*, September 15, 2021. https://www.nytimes.com/2021/09/15/books/new-books-race-racism-antiracism.html.

Harris, Elizabeth A. "People Are Marching against Racism. They're Also Reading about It." *New York Times*, June 5, 2020. https://www.nytimes.com/2020/06/05/books/antiracism-books-race-racism.html.

Harrison, Da'Shaun. "In Grief." *Scalawag*, May 5, 2022. https://scalawagmagazine.org/2022/05/dashaun-harrison-healing/.

Hartman, Saidiya. "Intimate History, Radical Narrative." *Journal of African American History* 106, no. 1 (2021): 127–35.

Hartman, Saidiya. *Lose Your Mother: A Journey along the Atlantic Slave Route*. New York: Farrar, Straus and Giroux, 2007.

Hartman, Saidiya. *Scenes of Subjection: Terror, Slavery, and Self-Making in Nineteenth-Century America*. New York: Oxford University Press, 1997.

Hartman, Saidiya. "Venus in Two Acts." *Small Axe: A Caribbean Journal of Criticism* 12, no. 2 (2008): 1–14.

Hartman, Saidiya. *Wayward Lives, Beautiful Experiments: Intimate Histories of Social Upheaval*. New York: W. W. Norton, 2019.

Hemmings, Clare. *Why Stories Matter: The Political Grammar of Feminist Theory*. Durham, NC: Duke University Press, 2011.

Hill Collins, Patricia. *Black Feminist Thought: Knowledge, Consciousness, and the Politics of Empowerment*. New York: Routledge, 1990.

Hill Collins, Patricia. "Learning from the Outsider Within: The Sociological Significance of Black Feminist Thought." *Social Problems* 33, no. 6 (1986): S14–S32.

Hine, Darlene Clark. "Rape and the Inner Lives of Black Women in the Middle West." *Signs: A Journal of Women in Culture and Society* 14, no. 4 (1989): 912–20.

Hirsch, Marianne. *Family Frames: Photography, Narrative, and Postmemory*. Cambridge, MA: Harvard University Press, 1997.

Holloway, Karla F.C. *Passed On: African American Mourning Stories*. Durham, NC: Duke University Press, 2002.

Hong, Grace. "'The Future of Our Worlds': Black Feminism and the Politics of Knowledge in the University under Globalization." *Meridians: Feminism, Race, Transnationalism* 8, no. 2 (2008): 95–115.

hooks, bell. "Selling Hot Pussy." In *Black Looks: Race and Representation*. New York: Routledge, 2014.

Howe, Marie. *What the Living Do*. New York: W. W. Norton, 1999.

Hull, Akasha (Gloria T.), Patricia Bell-Scott, and Barbara Smith, eds. *All the Women Are White, All the Blacks Are Men, But Some of Us Are Brave: Black Women's Studies*. Old Westbury, NY: Feminist Press, 1993.

Jackson, Lauren Michele. "What Is an Anti-racist Reading List For?" Vulture, *New York Magazine*, June 4, 2020. https://www.vulture.com/2020/06/anti -racist-reading-lists-what-are-they-for.html.

Kuhn, Annette. *Family Secrets: Acts of Memory and Imagination*. New York: Verso Books, 2002.

Leigh, Simone, Amy Sherald, and Lorna Simpson. "'I Want to Explore the Wonder of What It Is to Be a Black American.'" *New York Times*, December 8, 2019. https://www.nytimes.com/interactive/2019/10/08/magazine/black -women-artists-conversation.html.

Levine, Philip. *What Work Is*. New York: Knopf, 1992.

Lewis, Sarah Elizabeth. "Where Are the Photos of People Dying of Covid?" *New York Times*, May 1, 2020. https://www.nytimes.com/2020/05/01 /opinion/coronavirus-photography.html.

Lorde, Audre. *Zami: A New Spelling of My Name*. Berkeley: Crossing Press, 2016.

Lordi, Emily. "Between the World and the Addressee: Epistolary Nonfiction by Ta-Nehisi Coates and His Peers." *CLA Journal* 60, no. 4 (2017): 434–47.

Lugones, Maria. "Playfulness, 'World'-Travelling, and Loving Perception." *Hypatia: A Journal of Feminist Philosophy* 2, no. 2 (1987): 3–19.

McClain, Dani. "As a Black Mother, My Parenting Is Always Political." *Nation*, March 27, 2019.

McKittrick, Katherine. "Mathematics Black Life." *Black Scholar* 44, no. 2 (2014): 16–28.

Moraga, Cherríe and Gloria Anzaldúa, eds. *This Bridge Called My Back: Writings by Radical Women of Color*. New York: Kitchen Table Women of Color Press, 1983.

Morgan, Joan. *When Chickenheads Come Home to Roost: A Hip-Hop Feminist Breaks It Down*. New York: Simon and Schuster, 2000.

Morris, Natalie. "Black women write love letters to Black children in response to the trauma of racism." *Metro*, July 29, 2021. https://metro.co.uk/2021

/07/29/black-women-write-love-letters-to-children-to-tackle-trauma-of
-racism-15006123/.

Morris, Wesley. "The Videos That Rocked America. The Song That Knows Our Rage." *New York Times*, June 3, 2020. https://www.nytimes.com/2020/06 /03/arts/george-floyd-video-racism.html

Morrison, Toni. *Song of Solomon*. New York: Knopf, 1977.

Morrison, Toni. *Sula*. New York: Knopf, 1974.

Muñoz, José Esteban. "Vitalism's After-Burn: The Sense of Ana Mendieta." *Women and Performance* 21, no. 2 (2011): 191–98.

Nash, Jennifer C. *Birthing Black Mothers*. Durham, NC: Duke University Press, 2021.

Nash, Jennifer C. "On the Beginning of the World: Dominance Feminism, Afropessimism, and the Meanings of Gender." *Feminist Theory* 23, no. 4 (2022): 556–74.

Nash, Jennifer C. "*Wayward Lives*: Review." *American Historical Review* 125, no. 2 (2020): 595–97.

Nash, Jennifer C. "Writing Black Beauty." *Signs: A Journal of Women in Culture and Society* 45, no. 1 (2019): 101–22.

Nash, Jennifer C., and Samantha Pinto. "A New Genealogy of 'Intelligent Rage,' or Other Ways to Think about White Women in Feminism." *Signs: A Journal of Women in Culture and Society* 46, no. 4 (2021): 883–910.

Nash, Jennifer C., and Samantha Pinto. "Strange Intimacies: Reading Black Maternal Memoirs." *Public Culture* 32, no. 3 (2020): 491–512.

New York Times. "An Incalculable Loss." *New York Times*, May 27, 2020. https:// www.nytimes.com/interactive/2020/05/24/us/us-coronavirus-deaths -100000.html.

Okeowo, Alexis. "How Saidiya Hartman Retells the History of Black Life." *New Yorker*, October 19, 2020. https://www.newyorker.com/magazine/2020 /10/26/how-saidiya-hartman-retells-the-history-of-black-life.

Owens, Emily. "'We Have to Make Them Feel Us': Open Letters and Black Mothers' Grief." *African American Intellectual History Society Blog*, August 20, 2014.

Peck, Patrice. "To My Daughter, with Love." *New York Times*, March 2, 2021. https://www.nytimes.com/2021/03/02/us/mothers-daughters-letters.html.

Perry, Imani. *Breathe: A Letter to My Sons*. Boston: Beacon, 2019.

Perry, Imani. "Stop Hustling Black Death." The Cut, *New York Magazine*, May 24, 2021. https://www.thecut.com/article/samaria-rice-profile.html.

Phu, Thy, and Elspeth Brown. "The Cultural Politics of Aspiration: Family Photography's Mixed Feelings." *Journal of Visual Culture* 17, no. 2 (2018): 152–65.

Price, Melanye. "Please Stop Showing the Video of George Floyd's Death." *New York Times*, June 3, 2020. https://www.nytimes.com/2020/06/03/opinion /george-floyd-video-social-media.html.

Purnell, Derecka. "Grief over Time." The Cut, *New York Magazine*, January 31, 2022. https://www.thecut.com/article/sybrina-fulton-trayvon-martin -interview.html.

Quashie, Kevin. "A Flash of Light and Life." *Journal of African American History* 106, no. 1 (2021): 122–26.

Quashie, Kevin. *The Sovereignty of Quiet: Beyond Resistance in Black Culture.* New Brunswick, NJ: Rutgers University Press, 2012.

Rankine, Claudia. "'The Condition of Black Life Is One of Mourning.'" *New York Times Magazine*, June 22, 2015. https://www.nytimes.com/2015/06 /22/magazine/the-condition-of-black-life-is-one-of-mourning.html.

Ratcliffe, Krista. "Eavesdropping as Rhetorical Tactic: History, Whiteness, and Rhetoric." *JAC: A Journal of Composition Theory* 20, no. 1 (2000): 89–90.

Rich, Adrienne. "Notes toward a Politics of Location." In *Feminist Theory Reader: Local and Global Perspectives*, edited by Carole Ruth McCann and Seung-Kyung Kim, 177–81. New York: Routledge, 2003.

Samuels, Ellen. "Six Ways of Looking at Crip Time." *Disability Studies Quarterly* 37, no. 3 (2017). https://dsq-sds.org/article/view/5824/4684.

Scarry, Elaine. *On Beauty and Being Just*. Princeton, NJ: Princeton University Press, 2001.

Sehgal, Parul. "An Exhilarating Work of History about Daring Adventures in Love." *New York Times*, February 19, 2019. https://www.nytimes.com/2019 /02/19/books/wayward-lives-beautiful-experiments-saidiya-hartman .html.

Sewing, Joy. "A Letter to My Black Son about Trayvon Martin, 10 Years Later." *Houston Chronicle*, February 28, 2022. https://www.houstonchronicle.com /lifestyle/article/sewing-trayvon-martin-10-year-anniversary-16951657 .php.

Sharpe, Christina. "Beauty Is a Method." *e-flux*, no. 105 (2019). https://www .e-flux.com/journal/105/303916/beauty-is-a-method/.

Sharpe, Christina. *In the Wake: On Blackness and Being*. Durham, NC: Duke University Press, 2016.

Sharpe, Christina. *Ordinary Notes*. New York: Farrar, Straus and Giroux, 2023.

Singh, Julietta. *The Breaks*. New York: Coffee House Press, 2021.

Smith, Barbara, ed. *Home Girls: A Black Feminist Anthology*. New Brunswick, NJ: Rutgers University Press, 2000.

Smith, Troy. "Samaria Rice rebukes Tamika Mallory, others 'benefitting off the blood' of police brutality victims." *Cleveland.com*, March 16, 2021. https://

www.cleveland.com/news/2021/03/samaria-rice-rebukes-tamika-mallory
-others-benefitting-off-the-blood-of-police-brutality-victims.html.

Spillers, Hortense J. "Mama's Baby, Papa's Maybe: An American Grammar
Book." *Diacritics* 17, no. 2 (1987): 64–81.

Spires, Elizabeth. "Globe." *Poetry Magazine*, October 1978. https://www
.poetryfoundation.org/poetrymagazine/browse?contentId=34054.

Stewart, Kathleen. *Ordinary Affects*. Durham, NC: Duke University Press, 2007.

Taylor, Janelle S. "On Recognition, Caring, and Dementia." *Medical Anthropology Quarterly* 22, no. 4 (2008): 313–35.

Tillet, Salamishah. "Endless Grief: The Spectacle of 'Black Bodies in Pain.'"
New York Times, June 19, 2020. https://www.nytimes.com/2020/06/19
/arts/elizabeth-alexander-george-floyd-video-protests.html.

Tindal, Brenda. "'Its Own Special Attraction': Meditations on Martyrdom
and the Iconicity of Civil Rights Widows." In *ConFiguring America: Iconic
Figures, Visuality, and the American Identity*, edited by Klaus Rieser, Michael Fuchs, and Michael Phillips, 257–76. Chicago: University of Chicago
Press, 2013.

Trethewey, Natasha. *Memorial Drive: A Daughter's Memoir*. New York: Harp-
erCollins, 2020.

Walker, Alice. *In Search of Our Mothers' Gardens: Womanist Prose*. San Diego:
Harcourt Brace, 1983.

Ward, Jesmyn. "Witness and Respair." *Vanity Fair*, September 1, 2020. https://
www.vanityfair.com/culture/2020/08/jesmyn-ward-on-husbands-death
-and-grief-during-covid.

Wiegman, Robyn. *Object Lessons*. Durham, NC: Duke University Press, 2012.

Wilderson, Frank B., III. *Afropessimism*. New York: Liveright, 2020.

Williams, Patricia J. *The Alchemy of Race and Rights*. Cambridge, MA: Harvard
University Press, 1991.

Williams, Patricia J. "Gathering the Ghosts." *A Line* 1, nos. 3–4 (2018). https://
alinejournal.com/vol-1-no-3–4/gathering-the-ghosts/.

Williams, Patricia J. "On Being the Object of Property." *Signs: A Journal of
Women in Culture and Society* 14, no. 1 (1988): 5–24.

Williams, Patricia J. *The Rooster's Egg*. Cambridge, MA: Harvard University
Press, 1997.

Wines, Michael, and Erica Goode. "Cities Rocked by Past Protests Offer Lessons in What, and What Not, to Do." *New York Times*, August 19, 2014.
https://www.nytimes.com/2014/08/19/us/cities-rocked-by-past-unrest
-offer-lessons-in-what-and-what-not-to-do.html.

Wortham, Jenna. "The Woman Shaping a Generation of Black Thought." *New
York Times*, April 26, 2023.

Woubshet, Dagmawi. *The Calendar of Loss: Race, Sexuality, and Mourning in the Early Era of AIDS*. Baltimore: Johns Hopkins University Press, 2015.

Young, Kenya, and Sam Sanders. "A Black Mother Reflects on Giving Her 3 Sons 'The Talk' . . . Again and Again." *NPR,* June 28, 2020. https://www .npr.org/2020/06/28/882383372/a-black-mother-reflects-on-giving-her -3-sons-the-talk-again-and-again.

Adichie, Chimamanda Ngozi, 45
afropessimism, 12–13
album, the, 72, 74, 77–84
Alchemy of Race and Rights, The
    (Williams), 85–87, 99n6, 113n21
Alexander, Elizabeth: 2, 14, 16, 58.
    See also *Light of the World*; Tray-
    von Generation
Alexander, Michelle, 54–55
Alzheimer's, ix, xi, 2, 23, 71, 92
anti-racist reading, 18–19, 32, 55,
    109n22
anticipation: loss and, 2, 3, 7, 9, 23, 34,
    42, 51, 54, 56–57, 60, 63, 65–66, 96
Anzaldúa, Gloria E., 16, 17
archives: Hartman and, 11, 72, 78–82;
    Trethewey and, 31–32, 41–43, 45;
    Williams and, 84–86
"As a Black Mother, My Parenting Is
    Always Political" (McClain), 19

Bay, Mia, 15
beautiful writing, 3–6, 10–13, 15–24,
    29–31, 69–70, 72–75, 96–98
beauty: Alexander on, 7–8; Black
    feminist theory and, 10–12, 95, 97;
    Black motherhood and, 6–9, 11–12,
    95; Hartman on, 11, 79–82; Scarry
    on, 12; Sharpe on, 6–7, 9–12, 80

"Beauty of the Chorus, The" (Hart-
    man), 81
Behar, Ruth, 10–11
Bennett, Brit, 54, 109n23
Berlant, Lauren, 93
Between the World and Me (Coates),
    54–55
Bey, Marquis, 8
Black boys, 2, 7–8, 57–60, 93, 96
Black death (analytic), 7, 12, 18, 22, 35,
    39, 51, 54, 60–61, 96
Black Feminist Theory: beautiful
    writing and, 3–6, 8, 10–13, 15–24,
    30–31, 69–70, 72–75, 97–98; on
    beauty, 6–12, 79–82, 95, 97; on
    Black fatherhood, 93–95; on Black
    motherhood, 8–9, 20, 55–56, 93–
    96; on Black ordinary, 2–3, 8–11,
    22, 56, 61, 65, 68, 96–98; on care, 4,
    13, 21, 34, 36, 69–70, 74, 79, 94–95;
    contemporary, 4–6, 10, 13, 15–20,
    29, 46, 73, 96–97; collective proj-
    ect of, 13–16; living-with, 4, 20–24,
    29, 30–31, 34, 40, 45–46, 72–74,
    77, 96–98; on loss, 1–6, 8–10,
    12–13, 18–24, 29–31, 46, 54–56,
    64–65, 72–74, 96–98; markets for,
    16–20, 53–55, 97; public facing,
    14–20; university and, 15–17, 20, 22

Black Lives Matter, 1, 18–19, 32–34, 36, 52–55

Black motherhood: beauty and, 6–9, 11–12, 95; Black feminist theory on, 8–9, 20, 55–56, 93–96; loss and, 1–2, 6–9, 19–20, 51–53, 55, 57–58, 61, 31–32, 45, 55, 57–58, 65, 93–96; political symbol of, 2, 55, 65, 93–94, 96

Black paternal, 93–95

Black Studies, 16, 69, 76, 94, 95

Briggs, Laura, 103n36

Breaks, The (Singh), 55–56, 61–65

Breathe (Perry), 17, 51, 53, 58–60

Brown, Michael, 51–52

brown motherhood, 61–65

Bumpurs, Eleanor, 111n49

Campt, Tina, 14, 16, 73, 75–77, 115n54

care: Black feminist theory and, 4, 13, 21, 34, 36, 69–70, 74, 79, 94–95; ordinary: 8, 93, 95, 96

Chambers-Letson, Joshua, 14, 59

Christian, Barbara, 15, 21, 102n17

Coates, Ta-Nehisi, 54–55

Collins, Patricia Hill, 15, 102n11

controlling images, 3

COVID-19, 7, 17, 18, 32–35, 88, 90

"Condition of Black Life Is One of Mourning, The" (Rankine), 1–2, 19

crip time, 103n10

critical fabulation, 11, 78

Danticat, Edwidge, 106n3

disclosure, x, 4, 5, 11, 16

duCille, Ann, 17, 20

eavesdropping, 48–49, 51–55, 57, 59, 61

Ellison, Treva, 115n48

Eng, David, 3

evidence: Trethewey and, 41–46

fatherhood: Black, 92–95

Felzmann, Lukas, 83

Fleetwood, Nicole, 14, 16, 73–75, 77, 110n25

Floyd, George, 7, 32–35

Fulton, Sybrina, 51–53, 116n3

Gaines, Korryn, 111n49

"Gathering the Ghosts" (Williams), xii, 4, 69, 84–87, 99n5

Ghebreyesus, Ficre, 37–41

Gordinier, Jeff, 37

Gordon, Avery, 86

Griffin, Farah Jasmine, 15, 37

Griffin, Sarah Mantilla, 57

Gumbs, Alexis Pauline, 8

Halberstam, Jack, 112n3

Haley, Sarah, 111n49

Hamilton, Jack, 52, 55

Hampton, Mabel, 82

Harrison, Da'Shaun, 101n6

Hartman, Saidiya, 5–6, 102n6, 105n64; album and, 72, 73, 77–84; beautiful writing and, 11, 80–81, 112n3, on beauty, 11, 79–82. See also: *Lose Your Mother*; *Wayward Lives, Beautiful Experiments*

Hine, Darlene Clark, 101n7

Hong, Grace, 21–22

hooks, bell, 22, 103n28

Howe, Marie, 111–112n55

Image Matters (Campt), 75–77

In Search of Our Mothers' Gardens (Walker), 8, 16

In the Wake (Sharpe), 17, 69–70

intimacy: beautiful writing and, 4, 9–10, 16–18, 20, 75–76; letter and, 52, 53, 55–56, 58–61; loss and, 5, 9–10, 16, 18, 28, 31, 33–40, 46, 55–56, 65, 72–76; photograph and, 72–76, 81

Jackson, Lauren Michele, 19, 109n22

Jones, Martha, 15

Kazanjian, David, 3

language: beautiful writing and, 4, 10–11, 24; limits of, 31, 41, 69–70, 73–76
letter, the: Black Feminists and, 5, 51–61, 68, 108n9, 110n25; Coates and, 54–55; Perry and, 51, 53, 58–60; Singh and, 55–56, 61–65
Levine, Philip, 111n54
Lewis, Sarah Elizabeth, 35
life-making, 10, 11, 37, 92–93
Light of the World, The (Alexander), 25, 27–32, 35–41, 44–48
living-with: 4, 20–24, 29, 30–31, 34, 40, 45–46, 72–74, 77, 96–98
Lorde, Audre, 16, 17, 21
Lordi, Emily, 52, 53
Lose Your Mother (Hartman), 8, 55–56, 61, 63, 64, 65
loss: anticipation of, 2, 3, 7, 9, 23, 34, 42, 51, 54, 56–57, 60, 63, 65–66, 96; Black motherhood and, 1–2, 6–9, 19–20, 51–53, 55, 57–58, 61, 31–32, 45, 55, 57–58, 65, 93–96; collective, 18, 33, 35–36, 38–39, 60; memory and, 6, 31, 34, 44–46, 96; ordinary, 2–3, 5, 22, 24, 55, 56, 61, 65, 68, 75, 94–97; personal, 33–34, 36, 38–39; proximity to, 5–6, 9, 10, 16, 18, 22, 29–30, 31, 45–46, 61, 64, 65, 72–73, 76, 97; slow, x–xi, 3, 22, 23, 30, 56, 62, 64–65, 66, 68, 94, 96–98; spectacular, 1–3, 7–8, 22, 56, 58, 59, 75, 96–97
love, 18, 29, 34, 38, 40–41, 57, 63–64, 68, 95

magical thinking, 58
Marking Time (Fleetwood), 74
Martin, Trayvon, 51–52, 57–58, 116n3
masking, 2–3
materiality, 30, 32, 41, 45–46, 98
McClain, Dani, 19

McMillan Cottom, Tressie, 101n7
Memorial Drive (Trethewey), 31–32, 41–46
memory (analytic): imperfect, 6, 10, 31, 41, 44, 46, 77; loss and, 6, 31, 34, 44–46, 96
Moraga, Cherríe L., 16
Morgan, Jennifer, 79, 113n8
Morgan, Joan, 3
Morris, Wesley, 107n14
motherhood. *See* Black motherhood; brown motherhood
Muñoz, José Esteban, 91

"Notes toward a Politics of Location" (Rich), 13–14, 30–31

"On Love, Loss, and What Comes Next" (Sandberg and Alexander), 29
On the Beach (image), 82–83
ordinary: care, x, 8, 9–10, 93–96; life, x, 2–3, 11, 22, 58, 68, 79–81, 96–97; loss, 2–3, 5, 22, 24, 55, 56, 61, 65, 68, 75, 94–97; spectacular loss as, 1–3, 7–8, 22, 56, 58, 59, 75, 96–97
Ordinary Notes (Sharpe), 8, 9, 17, 105n64
Owens, Emily, 108n9, 116n5

Pauli Murray collection, 81–82
Perry, Imani, 14, 16, 17, 51, 53, 58–60
Price, Melanye, 107n14

quotidian. *See* ordinary

pandemic. *See* COVID-19
photograph, the, 5, 70, 72–74; Campt and, 73, 75–77; Fleetwood and, 73–75, 77; Hartman and, 72, 73, 77–84; Sharpe and, 69–70, 72; Trethewey and, 41–43; Williams and, 73, 81, 84–87
Pinto, Samantha, 116n3
property: community, 60–61, daughters as, 64, object of, 84–85

proximity: to loss, 5–6, 9, 10, 16, 18, 22, 29–30, 31, 45–46, 61, 64, 65, 72–73, 76, 97; to readers, 5, 10, 16, 46, 52, 55, 61, 75
privacy, 4, 6, 39, 56, 60, 76

Quashie, Kevin, 2, 102n15, 113–114n23, 114n42

Radcliffe Magazine, 84–85
"Radical Love Letter to My Son, A" (Griffin), 57
radical specificity, 30–31, 59
Rankine, Claudia, 1–2, 19, 109n22
Ratcliffe, Krista, 53
reading list. *See* anti-racist reading list
reckoning: racial, 7, 32, 34, 36
respair, 32, 34, 36
Rice, Samaria, 60–61
Rice, Tamir, 54, 60–61
Rich, Adrienne, 13–14, 30–31

Sandberg, Sheryl, 29
Scarry, Elaine, 12, 114n37
seduction: beautiful writing and, 5–6, 31, 53
Sewing, Joy, 57–58
Sharpe, Christina, x, 14, 16, 17, 96, 104n53; on beauty, 6–7, 9–12, 80; on Black motherhood, 6–7, 8–9, 11–12, 102n14; photograph and, 69–70, 72; on writing, 69–70
Samuels, Ellen, 102n10
Savage, Barbara, 15
Singh, Julietta, 55–56, 61–65
Spillers, Hortense, 8, 104n53, 113n8
Spires, Elizabeth, 46, 104n42
staying at the bone, 4, 97–98; Alexander and, 25, 27, 29–32, 35–41, 44–47; Trethewey and, 31–32, 41–46; Ward and, 31–36, 44, 45
Steward, Kathleen, 101n9

talk, the, 56–57
Taylor, Breonna, 110n26, 111n49
Taylor, Janelle, 99–100n1
tenderness, 18, 54; Alexander and, 46; maternal, 8, 63; ordinary, 10, 24, 94; paternal, 94–96; photograph and, 74, 81; Ward and, 33, 34, 36, 45
Till, Emmett, 19
Till-Mobley, Mamie, 19
Trayvon Generation, 7, 18, 100n3
Trethewey, Natasha, 14, 31–32, 41–46

undisciplined, 69
university, the: Black feminism and, 15–17, 20, 22

vulnerability, 7, 10–11, 18, 30, 31, 46, 94, 95

wake work, 1, 4, 51, 69–70
Walker, Alice, 6, 8, 16, 17, 64, 104n63
Ward, Jesmyn, 14, 31–36, 44, 45, 98
Warner, Michael, 93
Wayward Lives, Beautiful Experiments (Hartman), 11, 7, 77–84, 112n3
Wiegman, Robyn, 14
Wilderson, Frank, 13
Williams, Patricia J., 14, 20; on Black motherhood, 8; photograph and, 73, 81, 84–87; on privacy, 102n14; on writing, 5, 15. *See also Alchemy of Race and Rights*; "Gathering the Ghosts"
"Witness and Respair" (Ward), 31–36, 44, 45
witnessing, 18, 30, 32, 34–36, 41, 44, 46, 94
Woubshet, Dagmawi, 60

Young, Kenya, 56

www.ingramcontent.com/pod-product-compliance
Lightning Source LLC
Chambersburg PA
CBHW030604270326
41927CB00007B/1045